# DiGiTAL TYPE

Rockport Publishers, Inc.
Rockport Massachusetts

ROCKPORT
PUBLISHERS

Copyright © 1997 Rockport Publishers, Inc.

Distributed to the book trade and art trade
in the United States by:
North Light, an imprint of F&W Publications
1507 Dana Avenue
Cincinnati, Ohio 45207
Telephone: (800) 289-0963

Other Distribution by:
Rockport Publishers, Inc.
Rockport, Massachusetts 01966-1299

ISBN 1-56496-259-8

10 9 8 7 6 5 4 3 2 1

Designer: Stoltze Design

Printed in Hong Kong

First published in the United States of America by:
Rockport Publishers, Inc.
146 Granite Street
Rockport, Massachusetts 01966-1299
Telephone: (508) 546-9590
Fax: (508) 546-7141

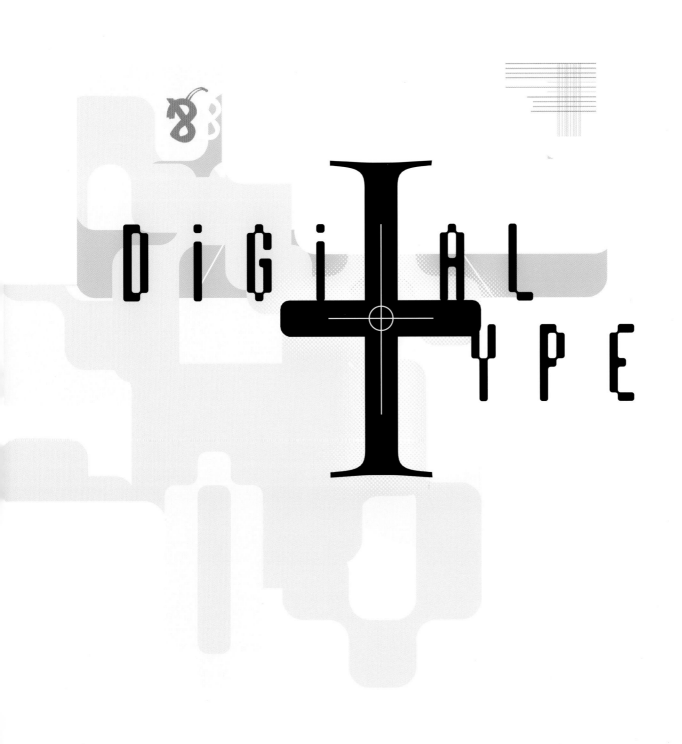

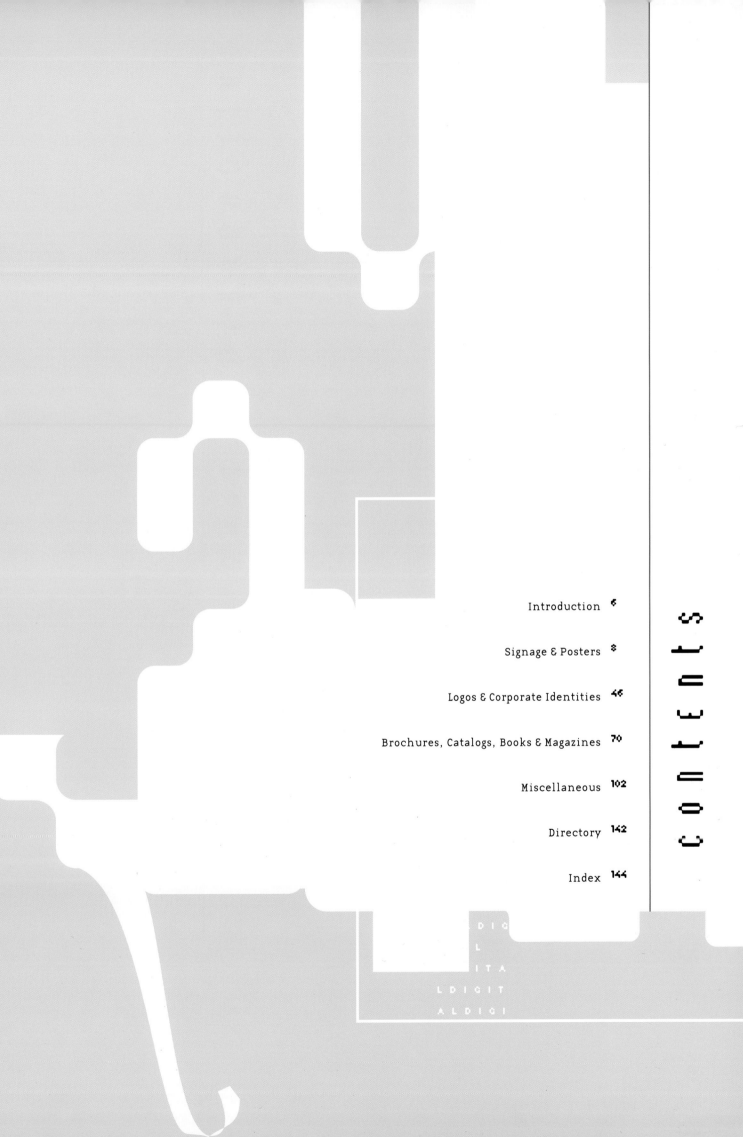

contents

introduction

The digital age has forever changed the visual landscape of graphic design. It has enabled the designer to try more ideas more quickly, and produce more complex and personalized solutions. Most notably, it has empowered designers to create their own images rather than relying solely on photographers or illustrators. Type itself can become the illustrative element.

Type as image—or in combination with other images—is nothing new. But today, with the utilization of drawing programs such as Adobe Illustrator and Photoshop as well as 3-D rendering programs such as Typestry, typography has become more alive than ever.

Rules have changed. The recent proliferation of computer-generated typefaces has eliminated the "safe list" of fonts from which designers should choose. Now there are literally thousands of typefaces and effects available which can combine to create millions of options. The challenge is to weed through the morass and arrive at the optimal solution without spending an eternity exploring different design possibilities.

This collection of recent work, submitted by designers from around the world, showcases a cross-section of projects which incorporate digital type that has either been designed or manipulated on the computer and used as a prominent aspect of the design. The examples range from highly personal work to more commercial projects with a specific message directed towards a broad audience.

Eliot Earl and Stephen Farrell represent a new breed of type designers whose promotional pieces uniquely capture the eclectic and surprisingly beautiful qualities of their fonts.

Carlos Segura masterfully integrates typefaces from his own foundry with real projects for business and culture reworking the modernist ethic into a truly contemporary hybrid of form and function.

Shuichi Nogami's letterform explorations do not use fonts at all. By combining different photographic images in Adobe Illustrator and Photoshop, Nogami creates formally stunning abstract letterforms.

Paula Scher's work for the Public Theater in New York lives in the culture of the street. The graffiti-influenced layouts are alive with the dramatic interplay of type and image, and evoke early woodcut advertisements from the beginning of the century.

The diversity of this collection clearly demonstrates that the use of the computer in design has evolved from a lumbering typesetting tool with its own techno-primitive aesthetic to a fast, sophisticated means of achieving a multitude of imaging tasks that no longer reveal the high tech process or origins.

As technology develops constantly, the full potential of digital typography grows exponentially. But as evidenced in this book, we always come back to the basic principles that make good design good design whether it comes from a rapidiograph or a Super-Duper Mac 200,000.

—Clifford Stoltze, Stoltze Design

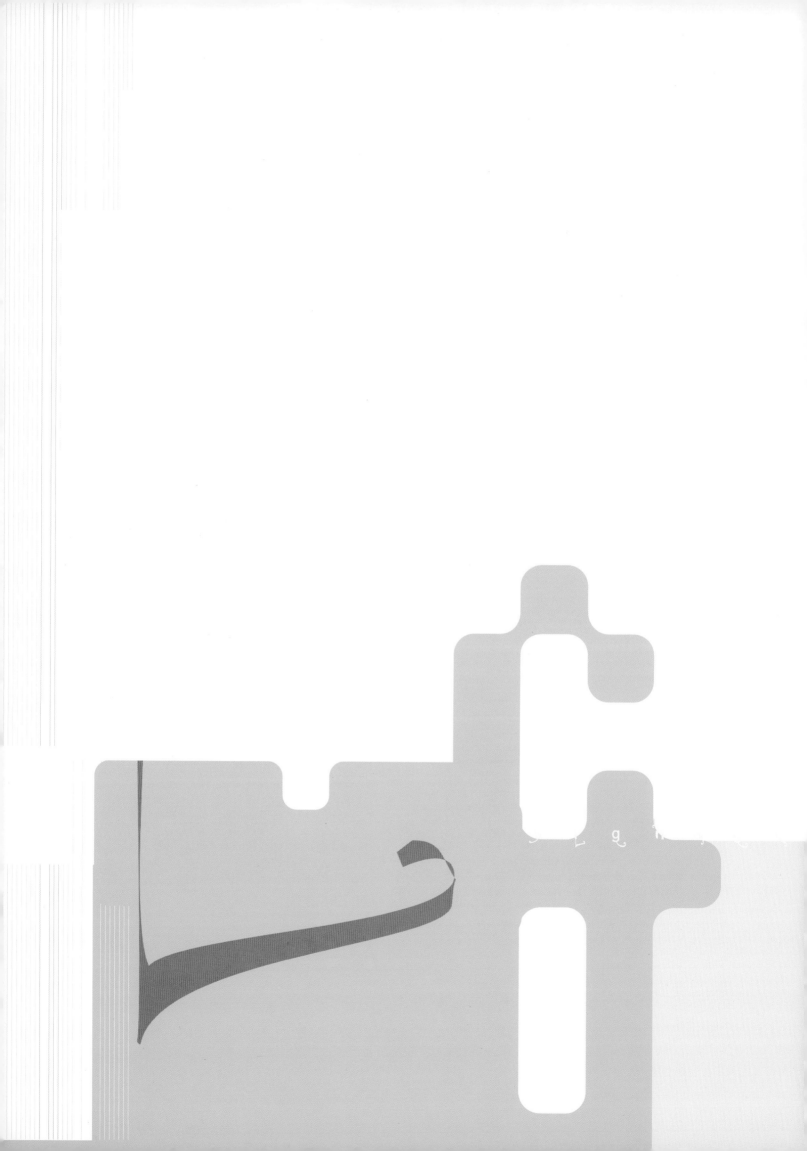

# signage & posters

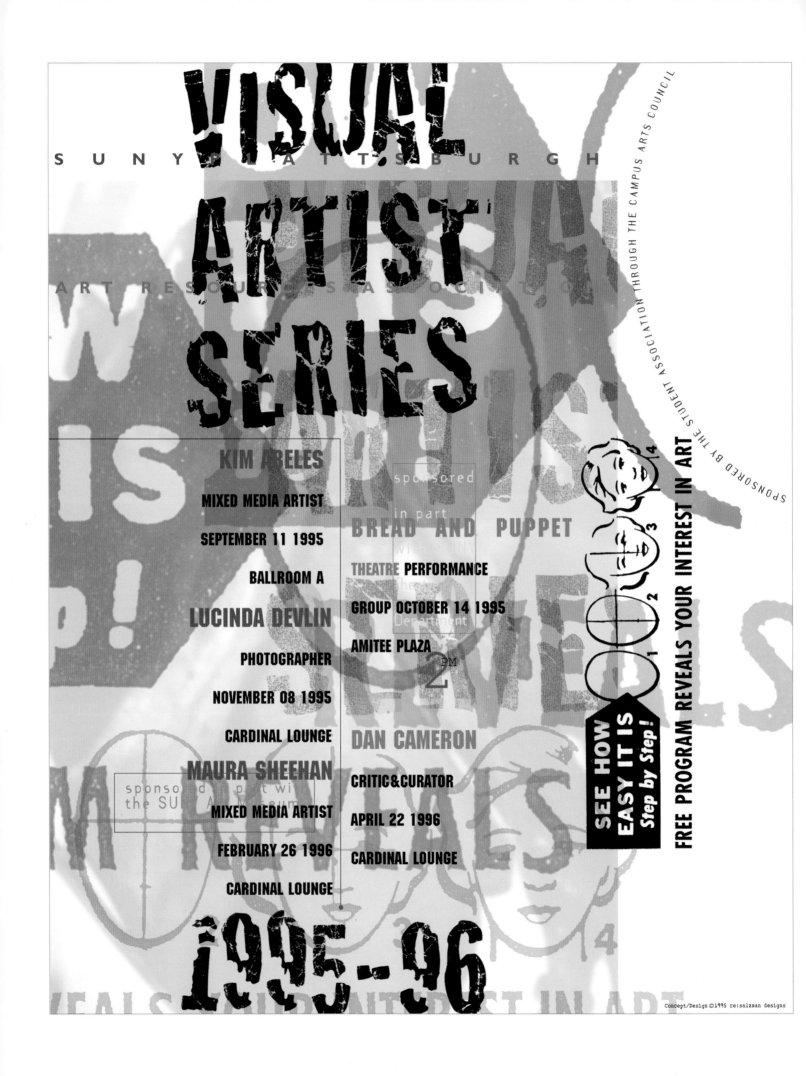

# VISUAL ARTIST SERIES

SUNY PLATTSBURGH

ART RESOURCES ASSOCIATION

**KIM ABELES**

MIXED MEDIA ARTIST

SEPTEMBER 11 1995

BALLROOM A

**LUCINDA DEVLIN**

PHOTOGRAPHER

NOVEMBER 08 1995

CARDINAL LOUNGE

**MAURA SHEEHAN**

sponsored in part with the SUNY Art Museum

MIXED MEDIA ARTIST

FEBRUARY 26 1996

CARDINAL LOUNGE

sponsored in part with SUNY Theatre Department

**BREAD AND PUPPET**

THEATRE PERFORMANCE

GROUP OCTOBER 14 1995

AMITEE PLAZA

2 PM

**DAN CAMERON**

CRITIC&CURATOR

APRIL 22 1996

CARDINAL LOUNGE

SPONSORED BY THE STUDENT ASSOCIATION THROUGH THE CAMPUS ARTS COUNCIL

FREE PROGRAM REVEALS YOUR INTEREST IN ART

SEE HOW EASY IT IS Step by Step!

**1995-96**

Concept/Design ©1995 re:salzman designs

DESIGN    Doug Bartow
PROJECT   *Less is Only More in Golf* poster
TOOLS     Macintosh
FONT      Franklin Gothic

This poster uses an image of Mies van der Rohe asleep on a park bench to question his overquoted statement, **"Less is more."** The designer sought to **activate the space** to emphasize this point.

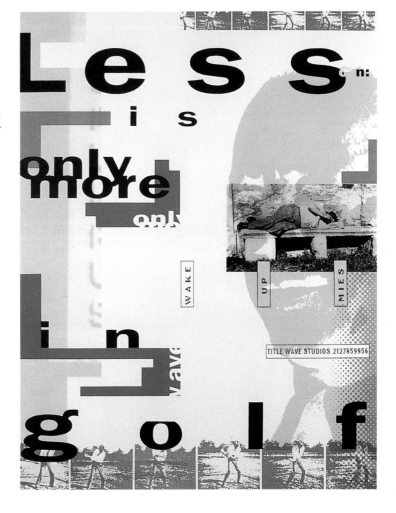

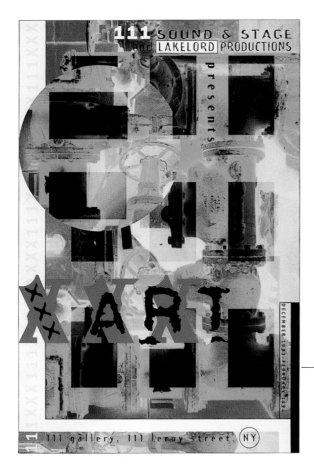

DESIGN    Norman Moore for Design Art, Inc.
PROJECT   Lakelord poster
CLIENT    111 Sound and Stage
TOOLS     Adobe Photoshop, QuarkXPress on Macintosh
FONT      Archaos, Caustic Biomorph

This is a **poster** for an art show.

DESIGN    Rick Salzman for re: salzman designs
PROJECT   '95–'96 Visual Artist Series poster
CLIENT    SUNY Plattsburgh Art Department
TOOLS     FreeHand on Macintosh
FONT      Crack House Xerox Distressed

The '95–'96 Visual Artists Series poster is an annual series sponsored by college art students. This year's theme was a **pun** of the comic book ads **challenging readers to test their artistic abilities.** The background is a blurred photo of a student's metal sculpture.

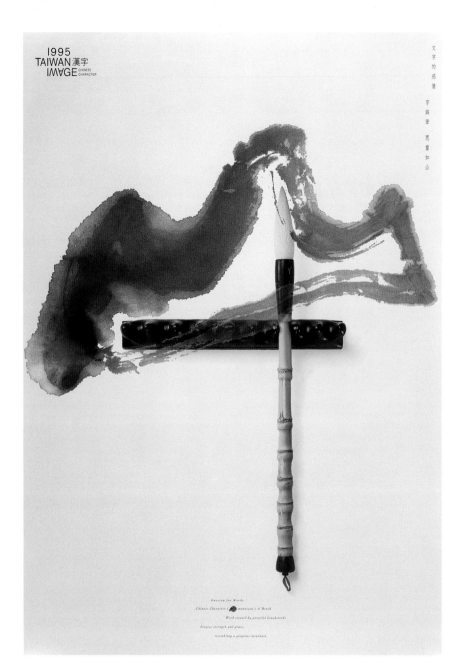

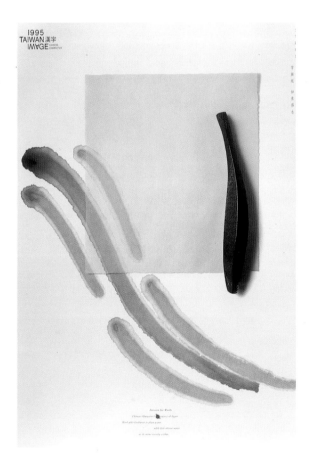

**DESIGN** Kan Tai-keung and Veronica Cheun Lai Sheung for Kan Tai-keung Design and Associates, Ltd.
**PROJECT** 1995 Taiwan Image - Chinese character (mountain, water, wind and cloud)
**TOOLS** FreeHand, Adobe Photoshop

This is a set of four posters specially **designed** for an invitation show.
Chinese calligraphy and traditional stationery show the **artistic and sentimental side of the Chinese character.**

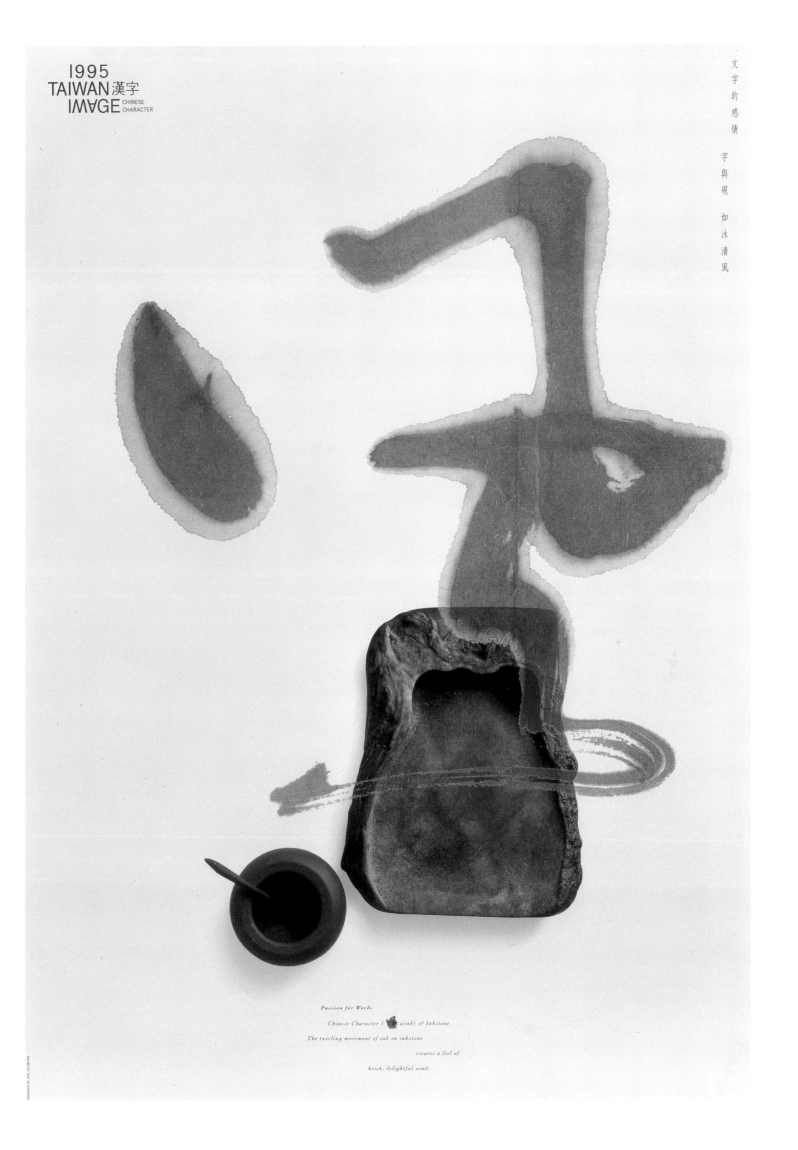

文字的感情

字與硯 如沐清風

# DESIGNER
# TODAY

PART 1 ▶ SHINNOSUKE SUGISAKI / KEN MIKI 〈 3.1 – 3.18 〉
PART 2 ▶ YOSHIMARU TAKAHASHI / TOSHIYASU NANBU 〈 7.4 – 7.16 〉
PART 3 ▶ KAZUAKI OHARA / SHUICHI NOGAMI 〈 10.18 – 10.29 〉
PLACE ▶ OSAKA CONTEMPORARY ART CENTER  GRAPHIC SPACE

DESIGN   Shuichi Nogami for Nogami Design Office
CLIENT   Osaka Contemporary Art Center
TOOLS    Adobe Illustrator, Adobe Photoshop on Macintosh
FONT     Franklin Gothic Demi

The letters and the photograph were compounded.

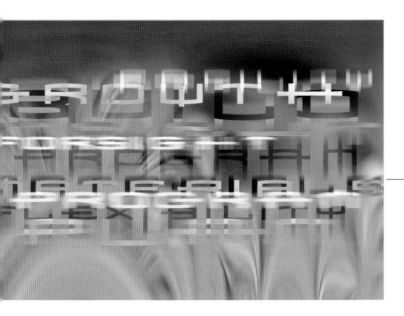

DESIGN   Tony Klassen for Segura, Inc.
PROJECT  MRSA
CLIENT   MRSA Architects
TOOLS    Adobe Photoshop on Macintosh
FONT     Mata [T-26] Font

This is an **illustration** of key words **altered** in Photoshop for a poster and mouse pad.

DESIGN   Robert Bak for Robert Bak
PROJECT  Bullet Proof Space
TOOLS    FreeHand, Adobe Illustrator, Adobe Photoshop,
         Kai's Power Tools on Macintosh
FONT     Empire BT

The type was made in FreeHand and **exported** as an Adobe Illustrator file. The **typographic layout** was also prepared in FreeHand. The backgrounds were designed in Photoshop with KPT filters.

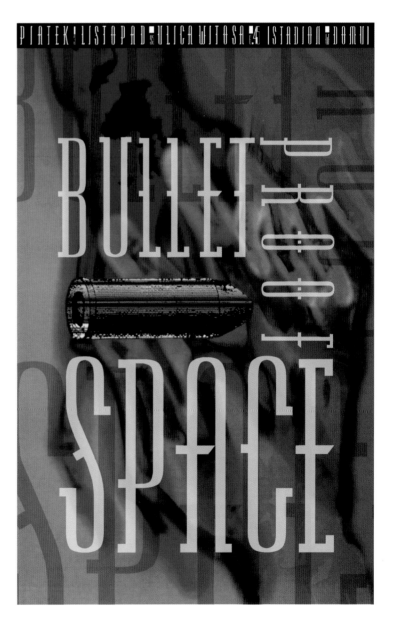

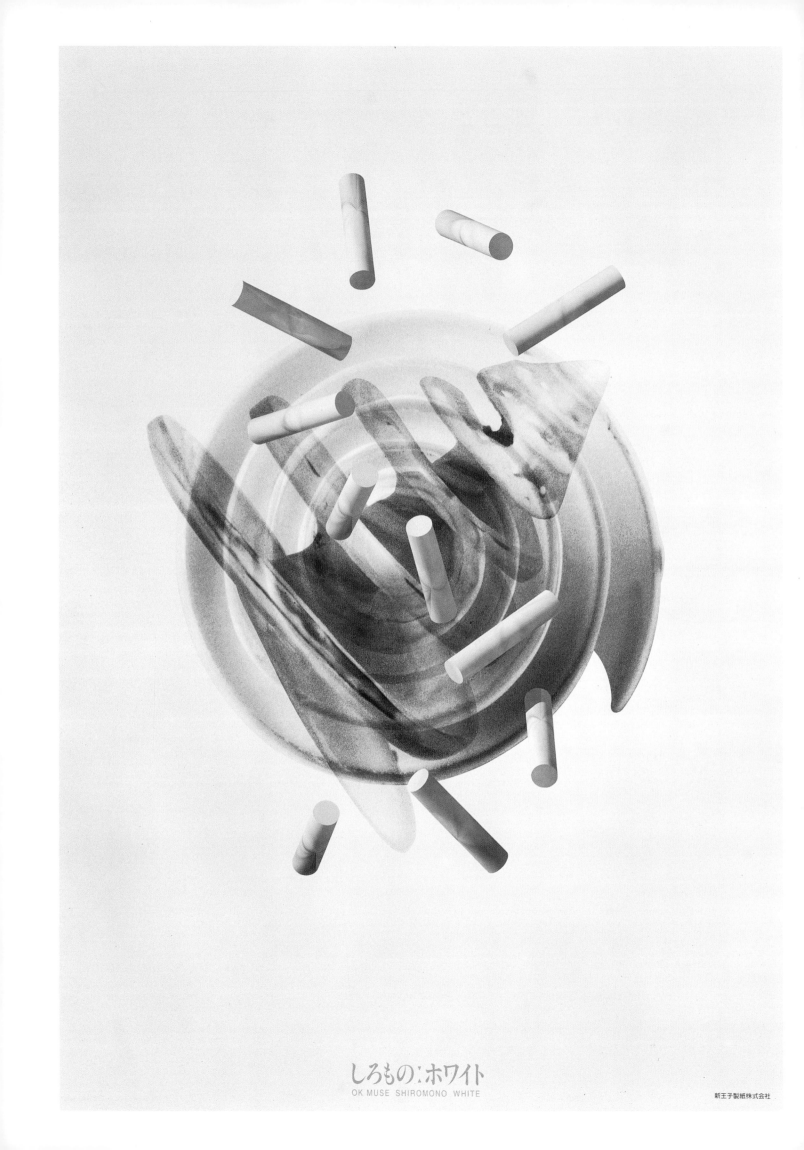

しろもの：ホワイト
OK MUSE SHIROMONO WHITE

新王子製紙株式会社

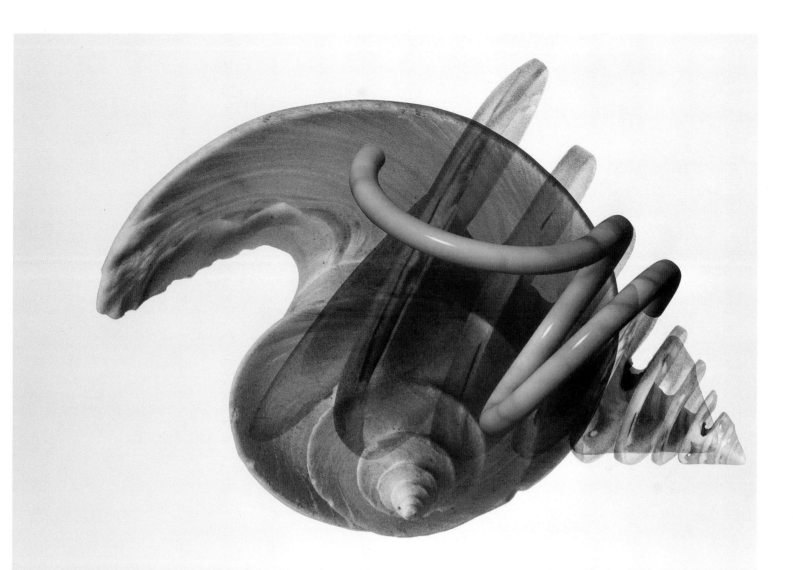

# DESIGNER TODAY

PART 1 ▶ SHINNOSUKE SUGISAKI / KEN MIKI < 3.1 - 3.18 >    PART 2 ▶ YOSHIMARU TAKAHASHI / TOSHIYASU NANBU < 7.4 - 7.16 >
PART 3 ▶ KAZUAKI OHARA / SHUICHI NOGAMI < 10.16 - 10.29 >    PLACE ▶ OSAKA CONTEMPORARY ART CENTER  GRAPHIC SPACE

DESIGN   Shuichi Nogami for Nogami Design Office
CLIENT   Osaka Contemporary Art Center
TOOLS    Adobe Illustrator, Adobe Photoshop on Macintosh
FONT     NIL

The letter *D* is **expressed through the combination** of different photographic images.

DESIGN   Shuichi Nogami for Nogami Design Office
CLIENT   New OJI Paper Co., Ltd.
TOOLS    Adobe Illustrator, Adobe Photoshop on Macintosh
FONT     NIL

The letter *O* was **expressed through the shapes** of the photograph in the design.

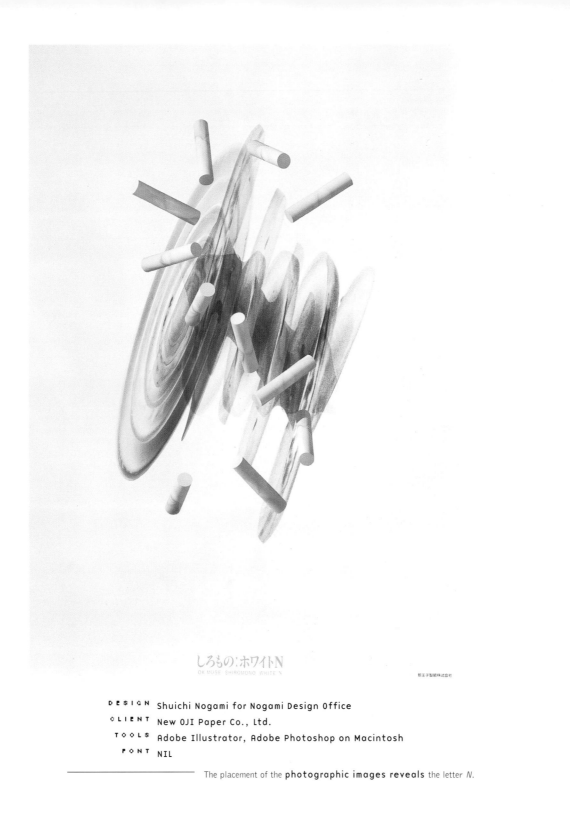

しろもの：ホワイトN
OK MUSE SHIROMONO WHITE N

OK王子製紙株式会社

DESIGN Shuichi Nogami for Nogami Design Office
CLIENT New OJI Paper Co., Ltd.
TOOLS Adobe Illustrator, Adobe Photoshop on Macintosh
FONT NIL

The placement of the **photographic images reveals** the letter *N*.

DESIGN Shuichi Nogami for Nogami Design Office
CLIENT New OJI Paper Co., Ltd.
TOOLS Adobe Illustrator, Adobe Photoshop on Macintosh
FONT NIL

The letter *S* is **expressed through** the use of photographic images.

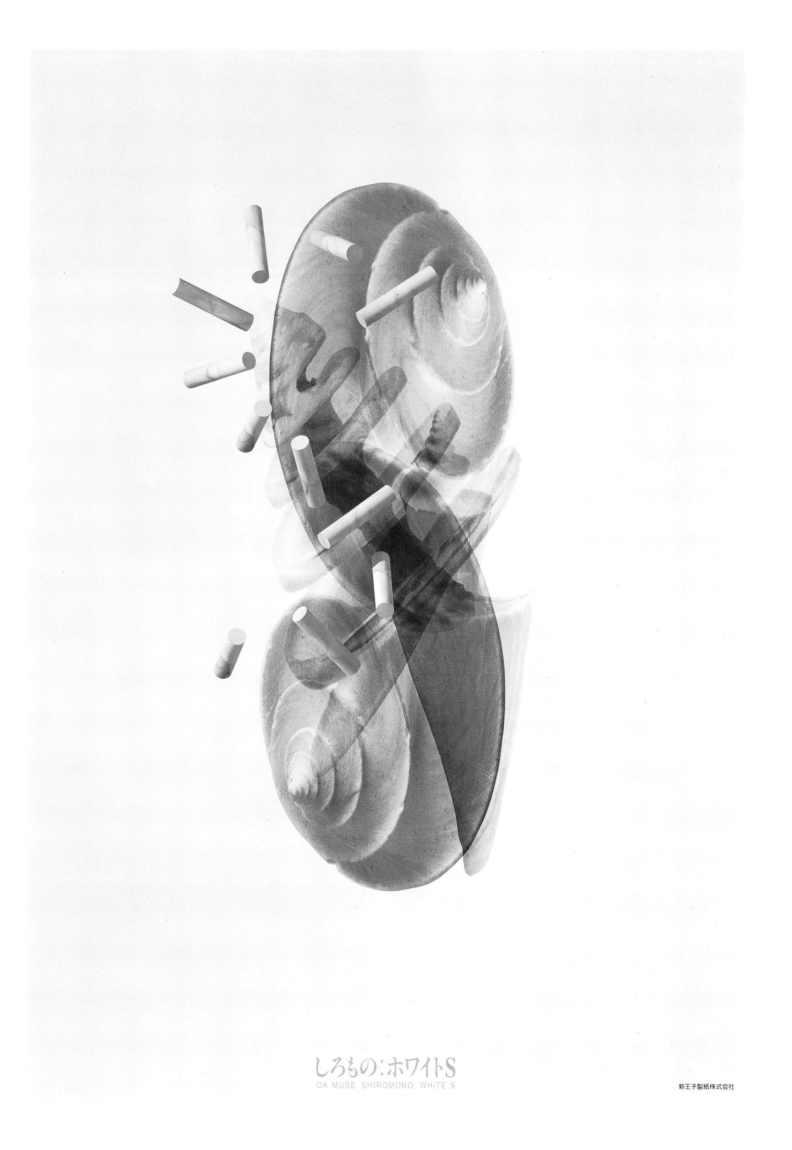

しろもの：ホワイトS
OK MUSE SHIROMONO WHITE S

新王子製紙株式会社

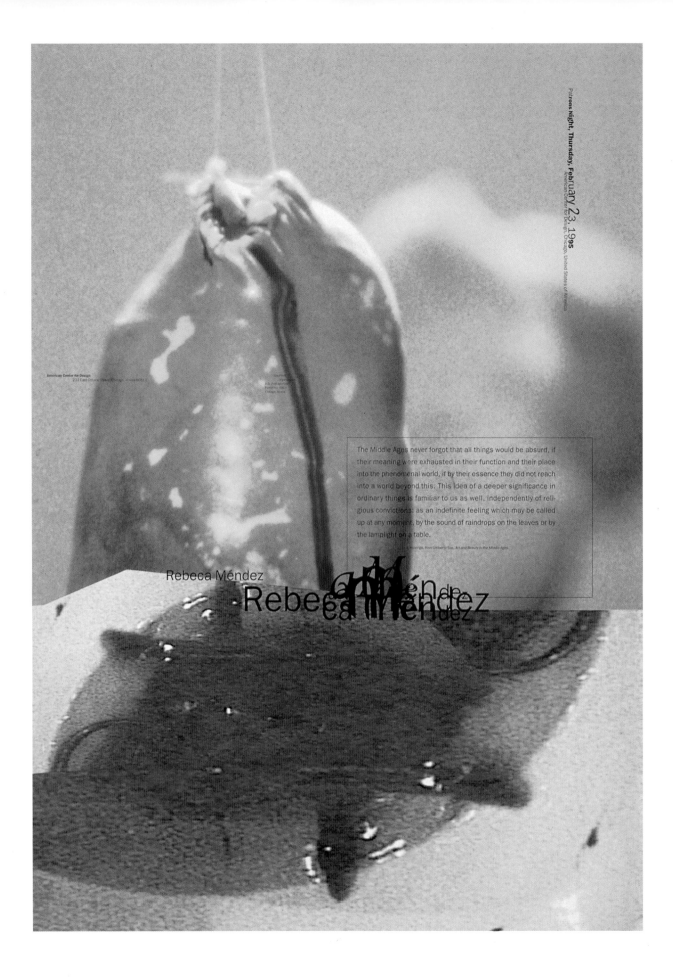

Patrons Night, Thursday, February 23, 1995
American Center for Design, Chicago, United States of America

American Center for Design
233 East Ontario Street, Chicago, Illinois 60611

The Middle Ages never forgot that all things would be absurd, if
their meaning were exhausted in their function and their place
into the phenomenal world, if by their essence they did not reach
into a world beyond this. This idea of a deeper significance in
ordinary things is familiar to us as well, independently of reli-
gious convictions: as an indefinite feeling which may be called
up at any moment, by the sound of raindrops on the leaves or by
the lamplight on a table.

Huizinga, from Umberto Eco, Art and Beauty in the Middle Ages.

Rebeca Méndez

Rebeca Méndez

DESIGN Rebeca Méndez for Rebeca Méndez Design
CLIENT American Center for Design
FONTS Perpetua and Franklin Gothic

The designer presented her design and art work for the ACD in Chicago. The poster includes imagery from **fine art videos, installations, and letterpress work.** The focus is the construction and deconstruction of **identity through boundaries,** both at an **individual** and at **an institutional level.**

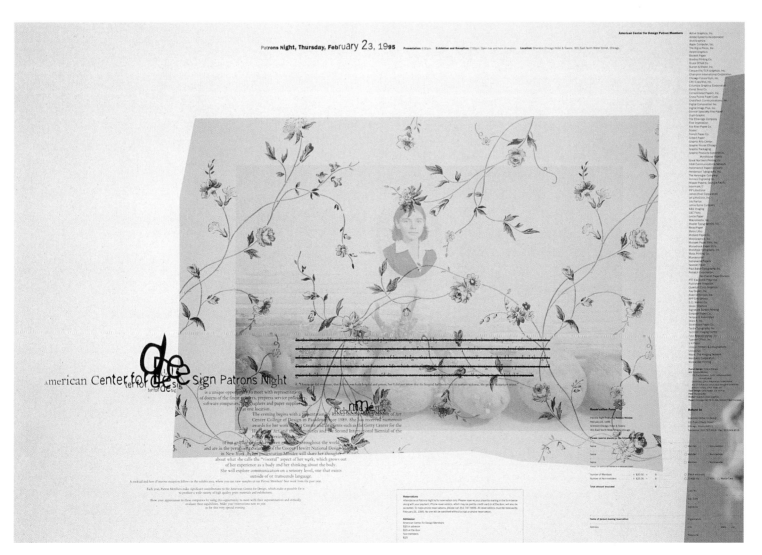

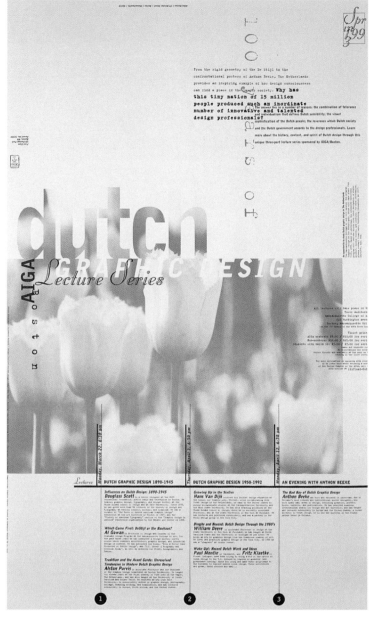

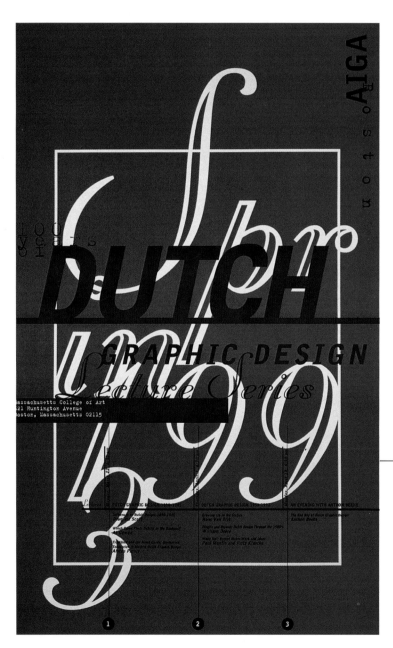

DESIGN    Clifford Stoltze for Stoltze Design
PROJECT   Dutch Graphic Design
TOOLS     AIGA-Boston
FONTS     Stuyvesant, Monotype Black, and Trixie

The **contrast between** a script (Stuyvesant), a sans serif (Monotype Black), and a typewriter font (Trixie) represents the **multiplicity of the Dutch design scene.**

DESIGN   Deborah Littlejohn
PROJECT   CalArts Poster and Mailer
CLIENT   California Institute of the Arts
TOOLS   Adobe Photoshop on Macintosh
FONTS   Data, Hubba Bubba

This poster is meant to represent an **electrically charged** atmosphere (CalArts) that emits students akin to birthing stars, still **connected to the mother planet by umbilical cords of energy.**

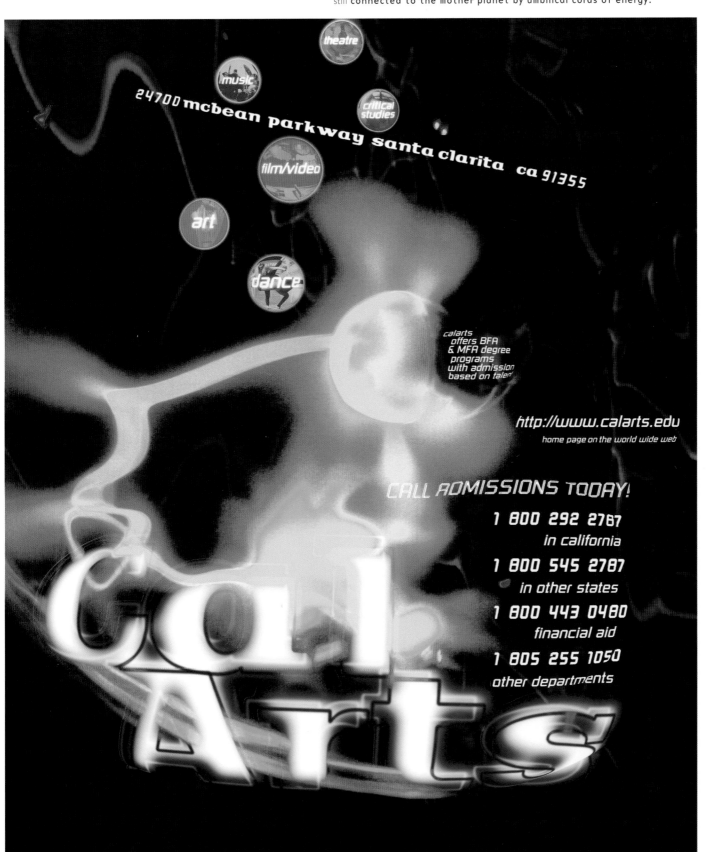

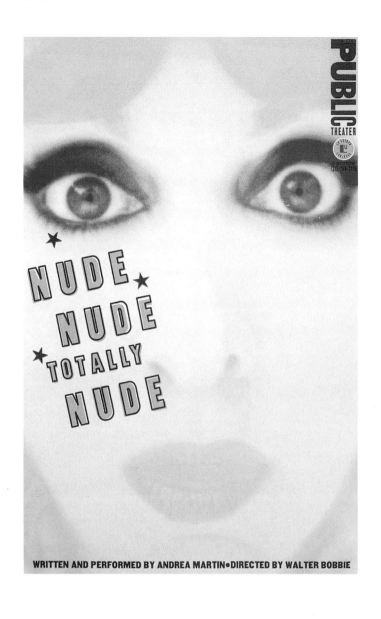

NUDE
NUDE
TOTALLY
NUDE

WRITTEN AND PERFORMED BY ANDREA MARTIN•DIRECTED BY WALTER BOBBIE

PUBLIC THEATER

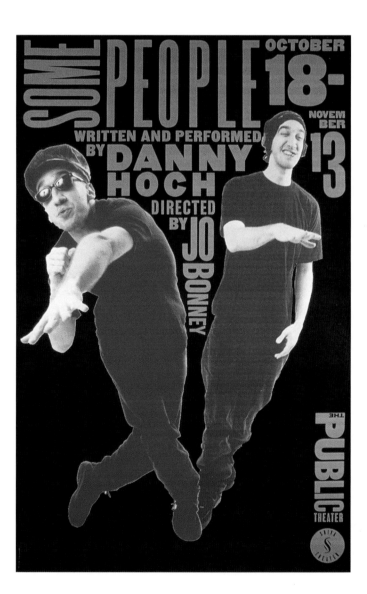

SOME PEOPLE

OCTOBER 18-
NOVEMBER 13

WRITTEN AND PERFORMED BY DANNY HOCH

DIRECTED BY JO BONNEY

THE PUBLIC THEATER

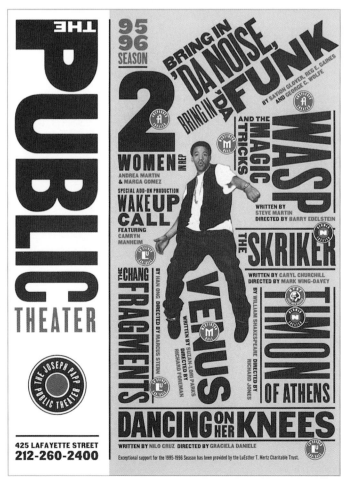

THE PUBLIC THEATER

425 LAFAYETTE STREET
212-260-2400

THE JOSEPH PAPP PUBLIC THEATER

95 96 SEASON

BRING IN 'DA NOISE, BRING IN 'DA FUNK
BY SAVION GLOVER, REG E. GAINES AND GEORGE C. WOLFE

2 WOMEN IN REP
ANDREA MARTIN & MARGA GOMEZ

SPECIAL ADD-ON PRODUCTION
WAKE UP CALL
FEATURING CAMRYN MANHEIM

WASP AND THE MAGIC TRICKS
WRITTEN BY STEVE MARTIN
DIRECTED BY BARRY EDELSTEIN

THE CHANG FRAGMENTS
BY HAN ONG DIRECTED BY MARCUS STERN

VENUS
WRITTEN BY SUZAN-LORI PARKS DIRECTED BY RICHARD FOREMAN

THE SKRIKER
WRITTEN BY CARYL CHURCHILL
DIRECTED BY MARK WING-DAVEY

TIMON OF ATHENS
BY WILLIAM SHAKESPEARE DIRECTED BY RICHARD JONES

DANCING ON HER KNEES
WRITTEN BY NILO CRUZ   DIRECTED BY GRACIELA DANIELE

Exceptional support for the 1995-1996 Season has been provided by the LuEsther T. Mertz Charitable Trust.

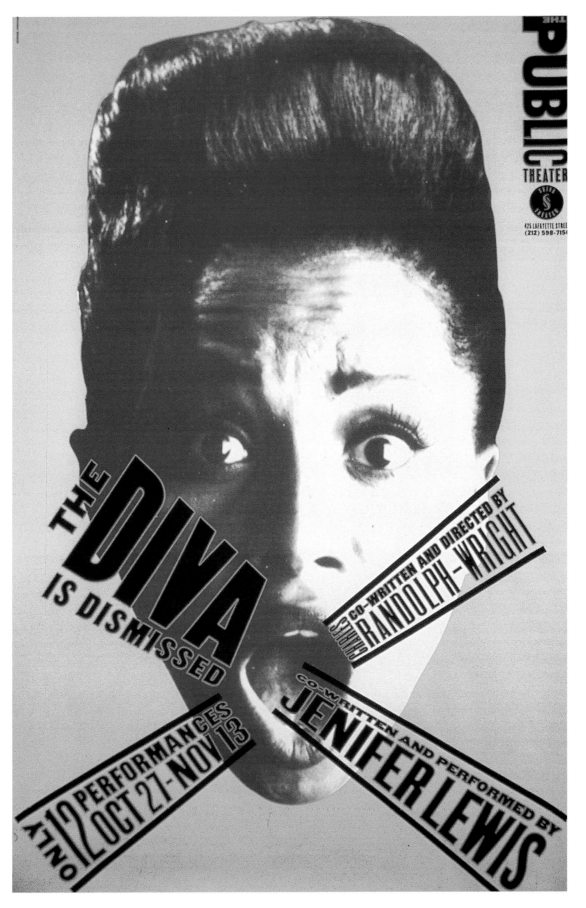

DESIGN Ron Louie, Lisa Mazur, and Paula Scher for Pentagram Design
PROJECT Public Theater poster series
CLIENT Public Theater
FONTS Morgan Gothic, Paulawood, Seriwood, E Ten, E Seventeen, E Twentyfive,
Wood Block Condensed, Alternate Gothic No. 2

———————————————— The varied but cohesive graphic language that Pentagram has developed reflects street
typography: It's extremely active, unconventional, and almost graffiti-like.

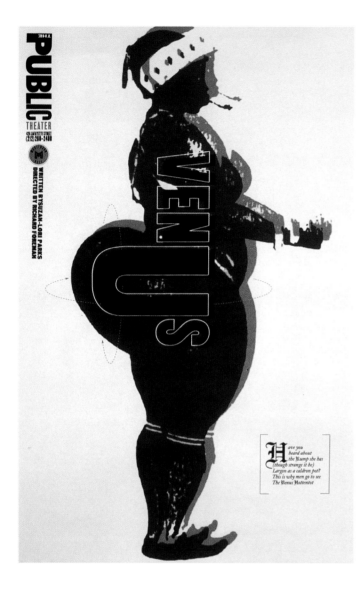

DESIGN Ron Louie, Lisa Mazur, and Paula Scher for Pentagram Design

PROJECT Public Theater poster series

CLIENT Public Theater

FONTS Morgan Gothic, Paulawood, Seriwood, E Ten, E Seventeen,
E Twentyfive, Wood Block Condensed, Alternate Gothic No. 2

The varied but cohesive graphic language that Pentagram has developed reflects street typography: It's extremely active, unconventional, and almost graffiti-like.

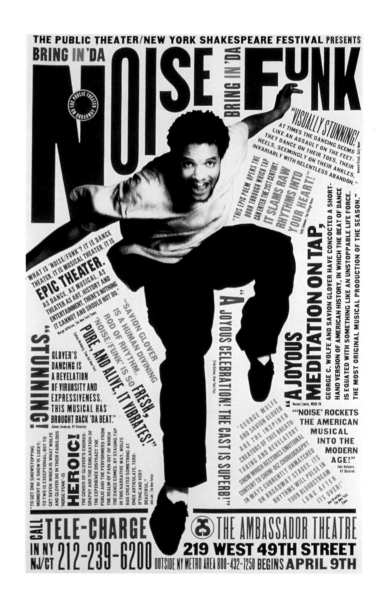

New Party, Institute For Policy Studies,
Present: A National Teach-In

The Rock The Boat Tour

Take Back America Before They Drown Us!

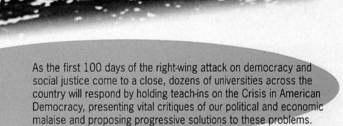

As the first 100 days of the right-wing attack on democracy and social justice come to a close, dozens of universities across the country will respond by holding teach-ins on the Crisis in American Democracy, presenting vital critiques of our political and economic malaise and proposing progressive solutions to these problems.

Through lectures, panels, films, and other events, the teach-ins will explore such topics as money in politics, sustainable development, democratic control of the economy, US. militarism, racism and xenophobia, and the need for a new progressive party in the U.S.

**Where:** *Universities and Colleges Across America*
**When:** *March 20 through May 6*
**Why:** *Because we Can't Afford Not To!*

DESIGN    Blaine Todd Childers for Todd Childers Graphic Design
PROJECT   *Rock the Boat* poster
CLIENT    The New Party
TOOLS     Adobe Illustrator, Adobe Photoshop

This poster uses type in a **photographic manner** to suggest a lifesaver **tossed out** to the American public **in the wake of a conservative landslide.**

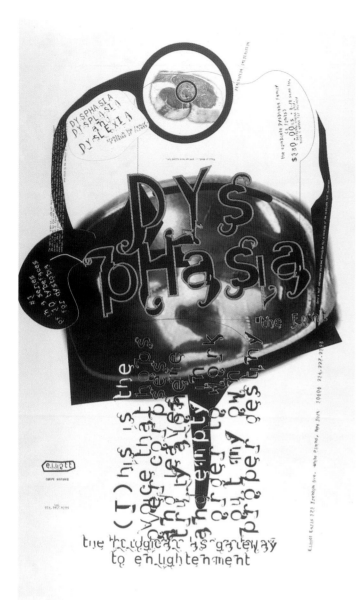

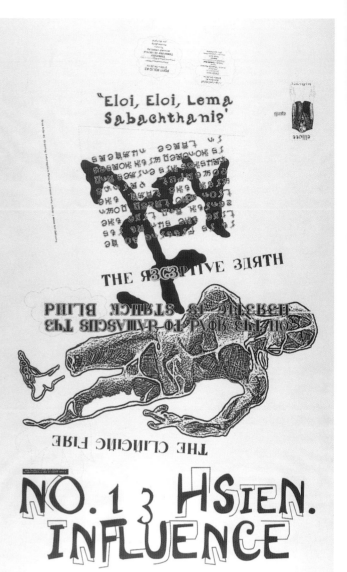

**DESIGN** Elliott Peter Earls for The Apollo Program
**TOOLS** Fontographer, Adobe Photoshop, FreeHand

This is a **series of posters** designed to promote The Apollo Program's type design.

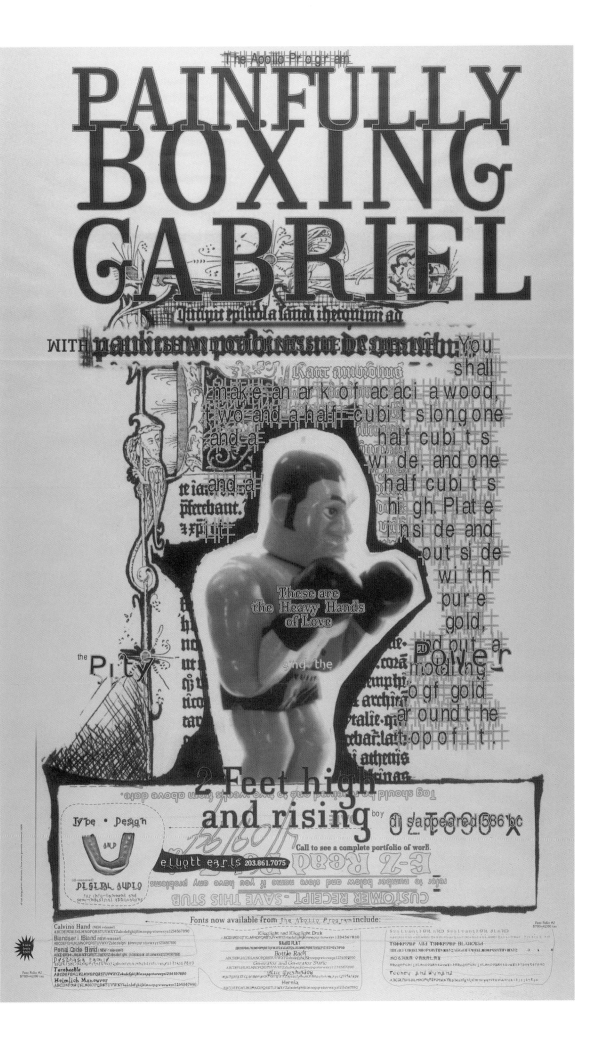

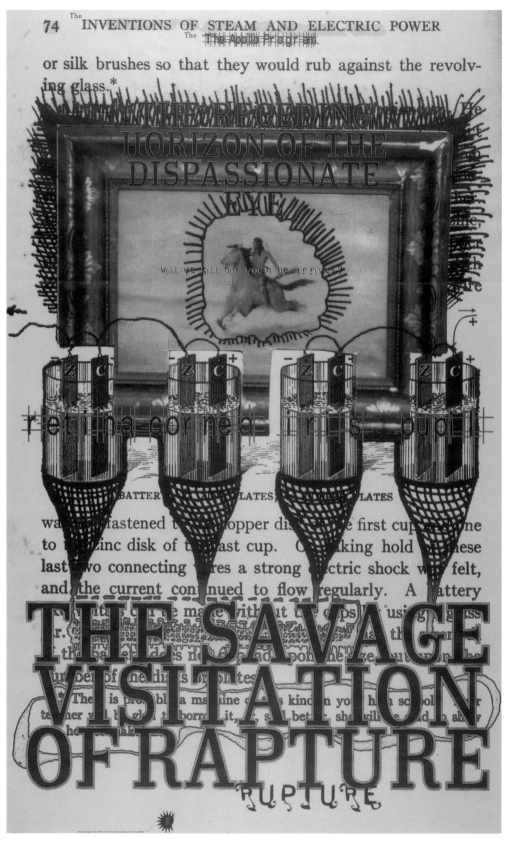

**DESIGN** Elliott Peter Earls for The Apollo Program
**TOOLS** Fontographer, Adobe Photoshop, FreeHand

This is part of a **series of posters** designed
to promote The **Apollo Program's** type design.

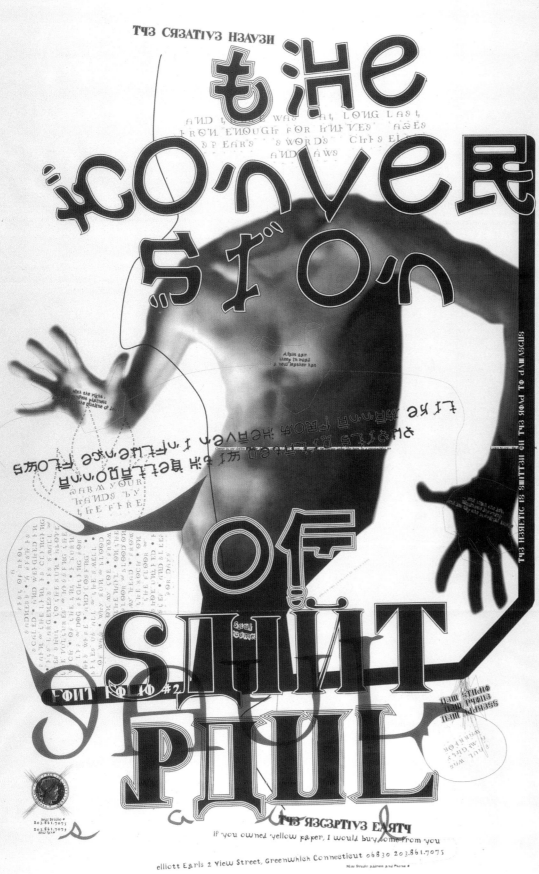

# the conversion of saint paul

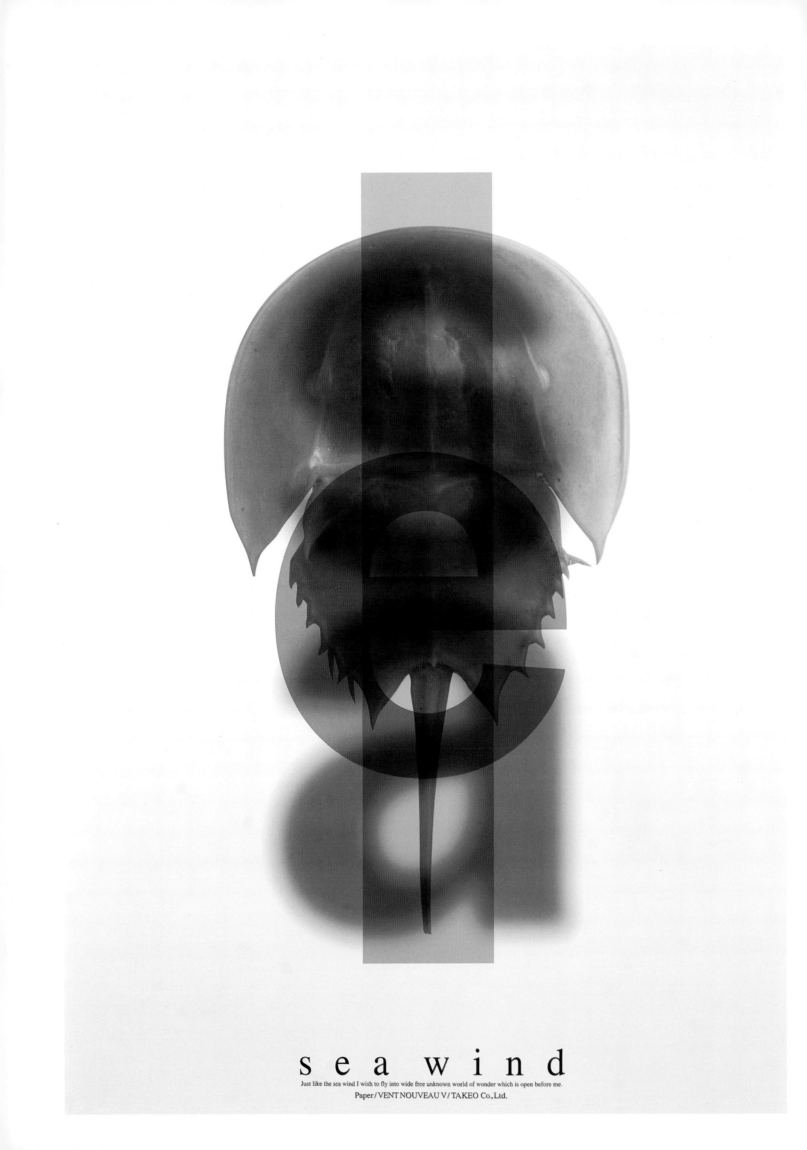

sea wind

Just like the sea wind I wish to fly into wide free unknown world of wonder which is open before me.

Paper / VENT NOUVEAU V / TAKEO Co., Ltd.

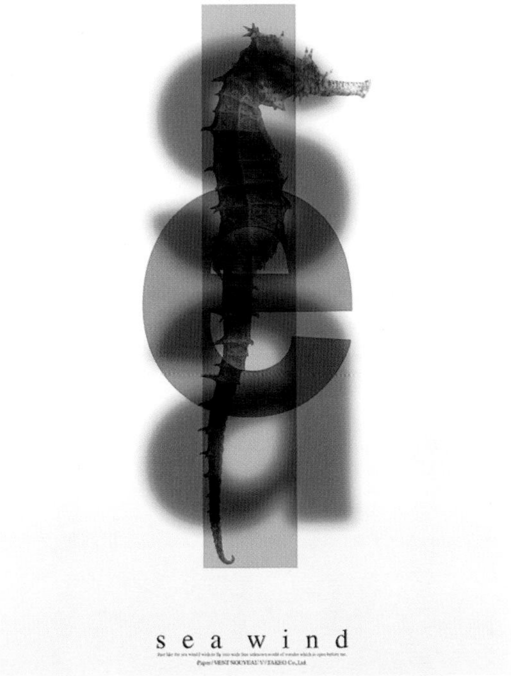


**DESIGN** Shuichi Nogami for Nogami Design Office
**CLIENT** Takeo Co., Ltd.
**TOOLS** Adobe Illustrator, Adobe Photoshop on Macintosh
**FONT** Franklin Gothic Demi

The letters in the word "sea" **were made to overlap,** and the **resulting shape was compounded** with the photograph.

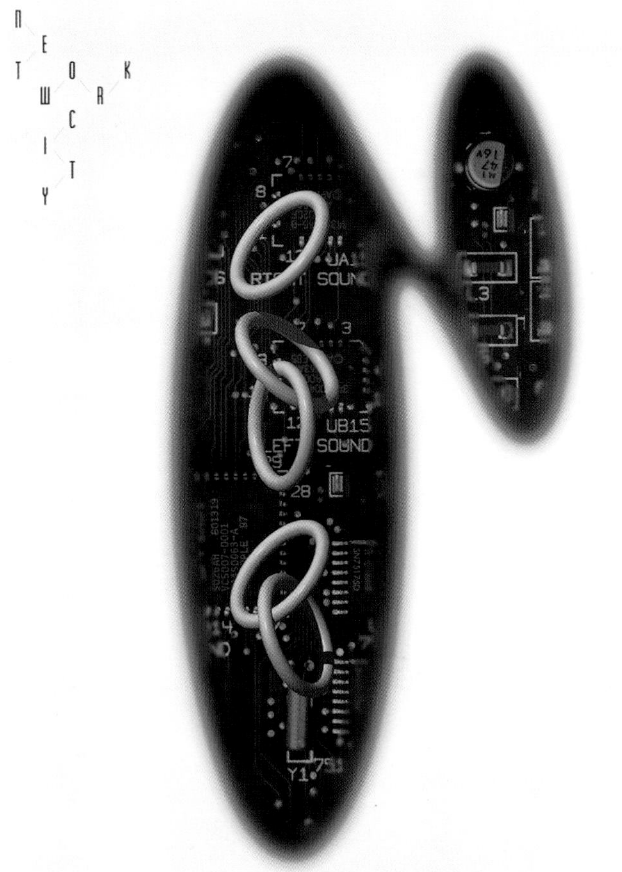


**DESIGN** Shuichi Nogami for Nogami Design Office
**CLIENT** Japan Graphic Designers Association, Inc.
**TOOLS** Strata Studio Pro, Adobe Illustrator, Adobe Photoshop on Macintosh
**FONT** NIL

*N* is **expressed through the design** rather than using the letter. The shape and photograph were manipulated to appear as a softened 3-D image.

**DESIGN** Shuichi Nogami for Nogami Design Office
**CLIENT** Takeo Co., Ltd.
**TOOLS** Adobe Illustrator, Adobe Photoshop on Macintosh
**FONT** Franklin Gothic Demi

Photographic images overlap the letters in the word "sea."

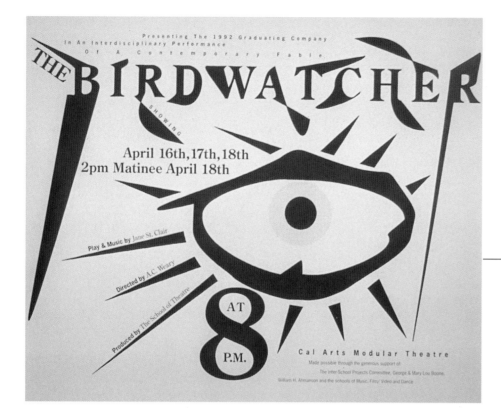

DESIGN James Stoecker
PROJECT CalArts Theatre poster
CLIENT Theatre Department
TOOLS FreeHand
FONT Century Old Style

The designer **created** this design after **reading the script** to the play.

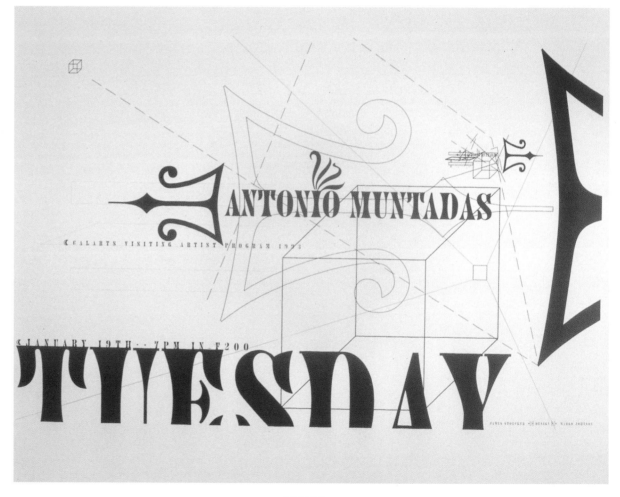

DESIGN James Stoecker
PROJECT CalArts: Visiting Artist poster
CLIENT CalArts Art Department
TOOLS FreeHand
FONT Juniper

Humor and seriousness **play out** in this **environmental artist's** work.

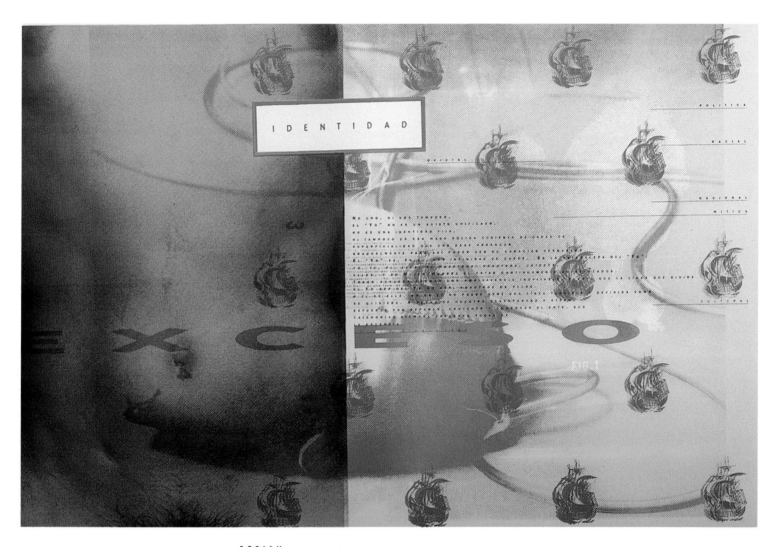

**DESIGN** Rebeca Méndez for Rebeca Méndez Design
**PROJECT** *America Now, 500 Years Later* poster
**CLIENT** Second International Biennial of the Poster
**FONTS** Franklin Gothic and Letter Gothic

This poster was created for an international invitational collection for forty posters held in Mexico City. The development of an identity is a very complex process, and any identity, whether is cultural, personal, national, political, or all of them together, is in constant state of change and mutation.

DESIGN   Fritz Klaetke for Visual Dialogue
PROJECT  Dance Month poster series
CLIENT   Dance Complex
TOOLS    QuarkXPress, Adobe Photoshop, FreeHand on Macintosh
FONT     Interstate

In each of the three posters, type and image **are combined** in different ways to **suggest an abstract** choreography.

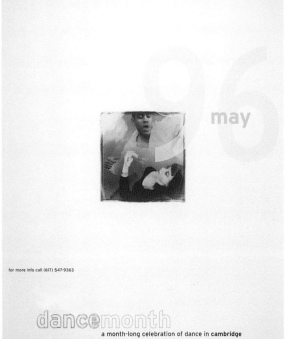

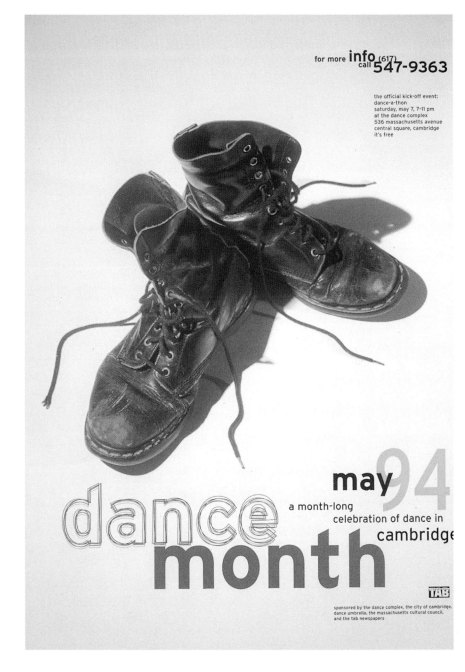

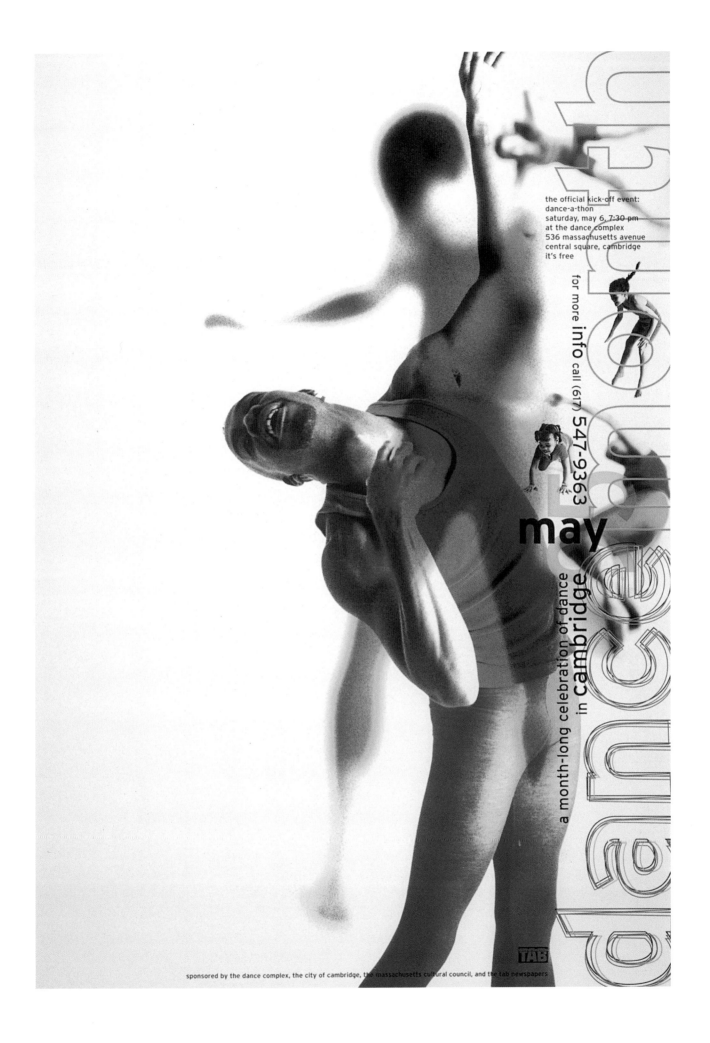

the official kick-off event:
dance-a-thon
saturday, may 6, 7:30 pm
at the dance complex
536 massachusetts avenue
central square, cambridge
it's free

for more info call (617) 547-9363

may

a month-long celebration of dance in cambridge

sponsored by the dance complex, the city of cambridge, the massachusetts cultural council, and the tab newspapers

**DESIGN** Clifford Stoltze and Peter Farrell for Stoltze Design
**PROJECT** Vaughan Oliver
**CLIENT** AIGA Boston Chapter
**FONTS** Scala, Folio, Poster Bodoni

Using images provided by Vaughan Oliver, a poster of **seemingly disparate images** and typography makes reference to Vaughan's **approach** to design. The record "label" design **pays homage** to the vinyl format.

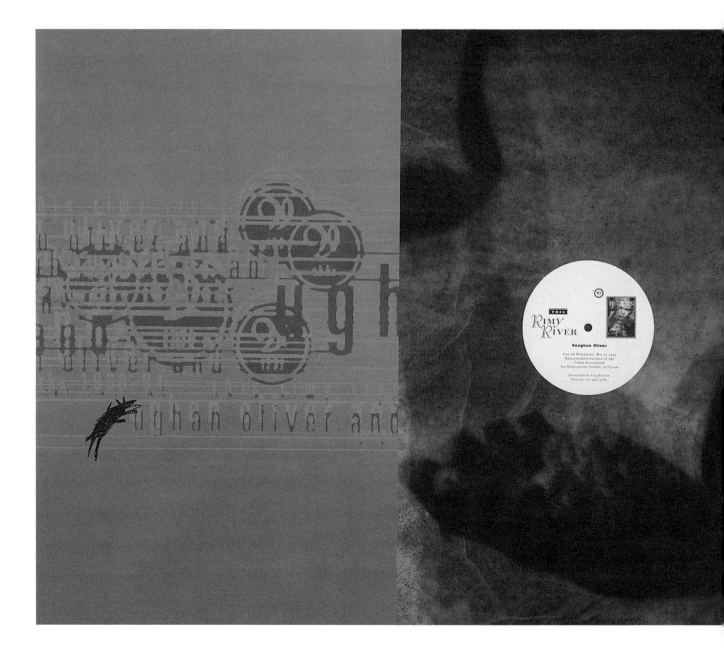

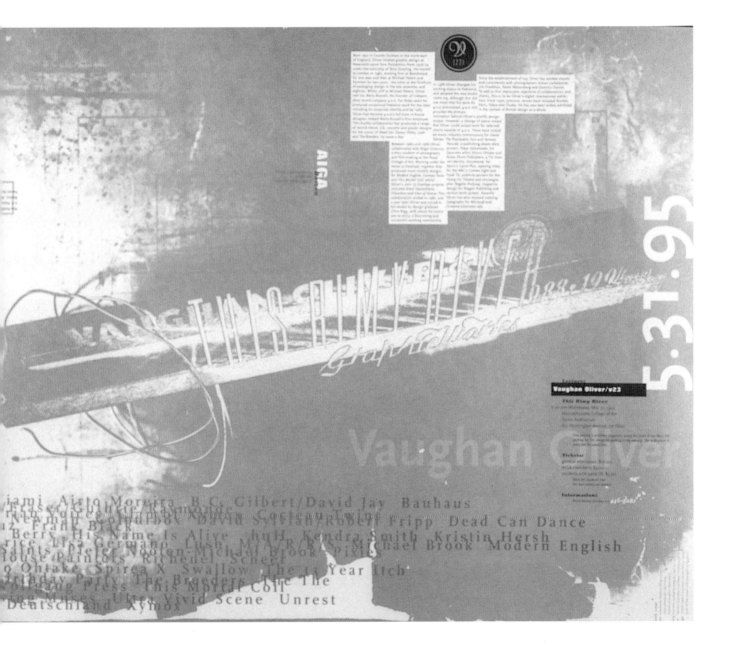

DESIGN  Blaine Todd Childers for Todd Childers Graphic Design
PROJECT  Dance On the Page
CLIENT  CalArts Dance School
TOOLS  Adobe Illustrator, Adobe Photoshop

This is a cover for a magazine designed for the CalArts Dance School.

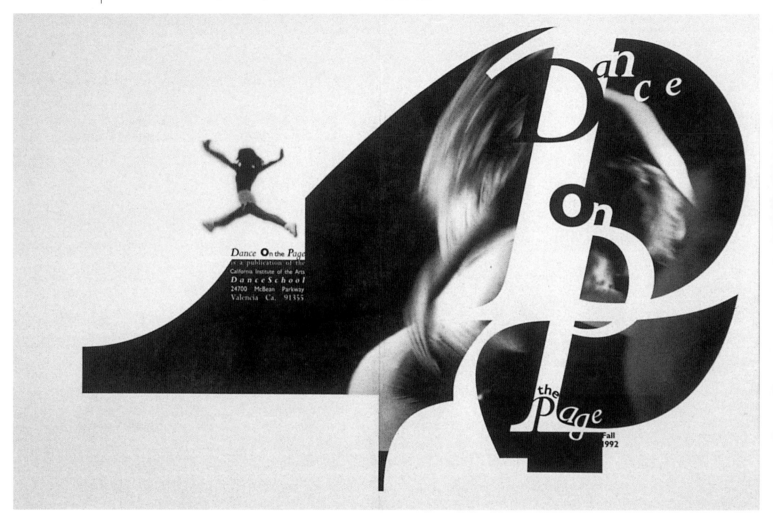

DESIGN  Deborah Littlejohn and Shelley Stepp
PROJECT  CalArts Spring Dance poster
CLIENT  California Institute of the Arts Dance School
TOOLS  Adobe Photoshop, QuarkXPress, FreeHand on Macintosh
FONTS  Perpetua, Cooper Black

The unstructured typography opposes images of a traditional dance recital performed in the evening hours, transforming energy, movement, and structure into chaos.

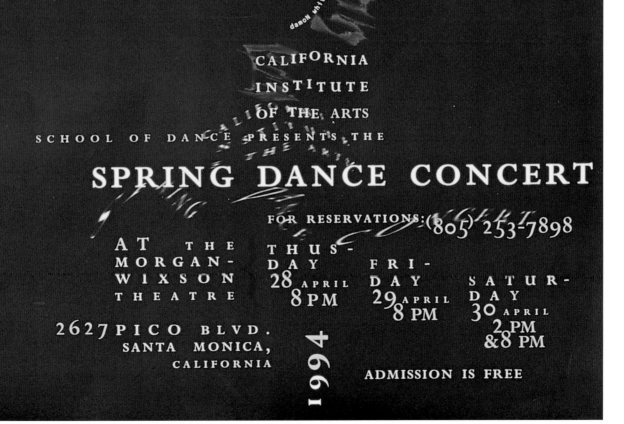

CALIFORNIA
INSTITUTE
OF THE ARTS
SCHOOL OF DANCE PRESENTS THE

# SPRING DANCE CONCERT

FOR RESERVATIONS: (805) 253-7898

AT THE
MORGAN-
WIXSON
THEATRE

THUS-
DAY
28 APRIL
8 PM

FRI-
DAY
29 APRIL
8 PM

SATUR-
DAY
30 APRIL
2 PM
& 8 PM

2627 PICO BLVD.
SANTA MONICA,
CALIFORNIA

1994

ADMISSION IS FREE

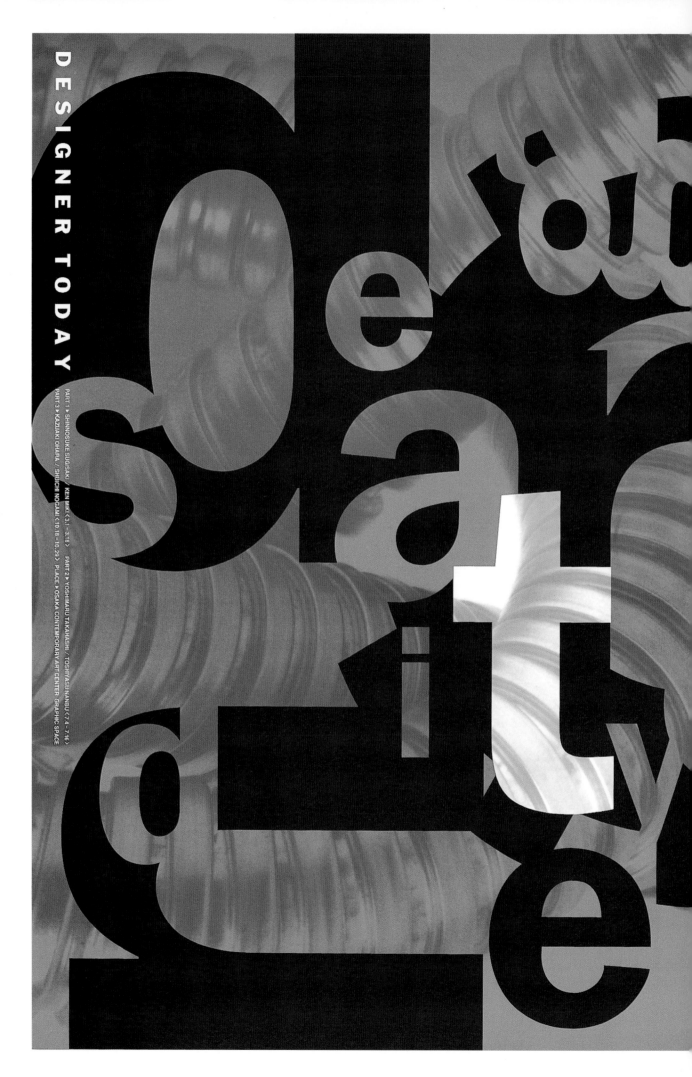

PART 1 ▶ SHINNOSUKE SUGISAKI／ KEN MIKI〈3.1 ─ 3.18〉
PART 3 ▶ KAZUAKI OHARA／ SHUICHI NOGAMI〈10.18 ─ 10.29〉 PART 2 ▶ YOSHIMARU TAKAHASHI／ TOSHIYASU NANBU〈7.4 ─ 7.16〉
PLACE ▶ OSAKA CONTEMPORARY ART CENTER GRAPHIC SPACE

DESIGN Shuichi Nogami for Nogami Design Office
CLIENT Osaka Contemporary Art Center
TOOLS Adobe Illustrator, Adobe Photoshop on Macintosh
FONT Franklin Gothic Demi

The **letters** and the **photograph** were compounded.

DESIGN Shuichi Nogami for Nogami Design Office
CLIENT Osaka Contemporary Art Center
TOOLS Adobe Illustrator, Adobe Photoshop on Macintosh
FONT Franklin Gothic Demi

The letter and the photograph were **compounded** for this design.

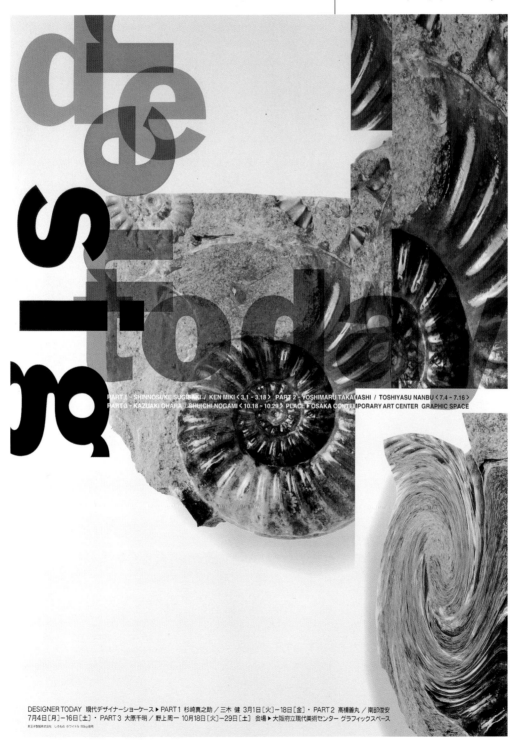

PART 1 · SHINNOSUKE SUGISAKI / KEN MIKI < 3.1 - 3.18 > PART 2 · YOSHIMARU TAKAHASHI / TOSHIYASU NANBU < 7.4 - 7.16 >
PART 3 · KAZUAKI OHARA / SHUICHI NOGAMI < 10.18 - 10.29 > PLACE ▶ OSAKA CONTEMPORARY ART CENTER GRAPHIC SPACE

DESIGNER TODAY 現代デザイナーショーケース ▶ PART 1 杉崎真之助／三木 健 3月1日［火］−18日［金］・PART 2 高橋善丸／南部俊安
7月4日［月］−16日［土］・PART 3 大原千明／野上周一 10月18日［火］−29日［土］ 会場▶大阪府立現代美術センター グラフィックスペース

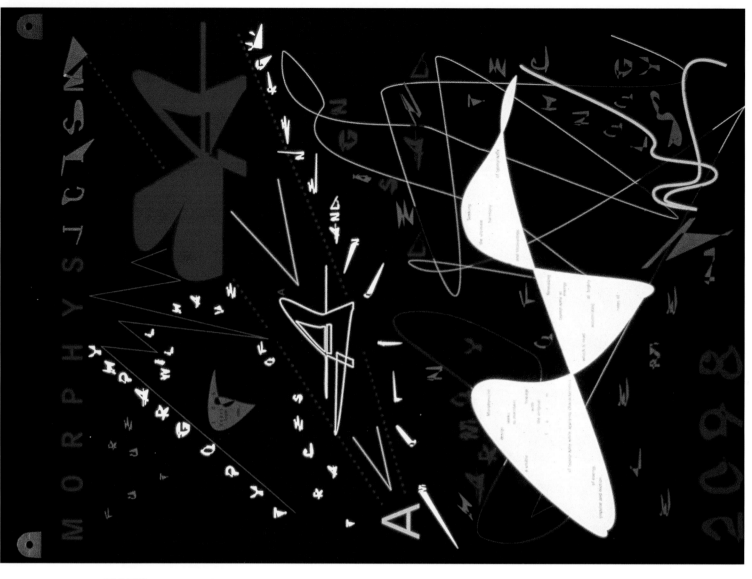

DESIGN     James Stoecker
PROJECT    CalArts poster: morphysicism personal project with type
TOOLS      FreeHand
FONTS      News Gothic, Bell Gothic

This piece was designed to **express the fluid dynamics** of typography today. It also **reflects** the information age's impact on design, **transmission, transgression, metamorphosis** of code, outline, type.

DESIGN     James Stoecker
PROJECT    Personal Elements of Earth series
TOOLS      FreeHand, Paste-Up
FONT       Futura

One of a series of posters proposed to **create awareness** of the environment by **conceptually working** from definitions and **phonetic structure.**

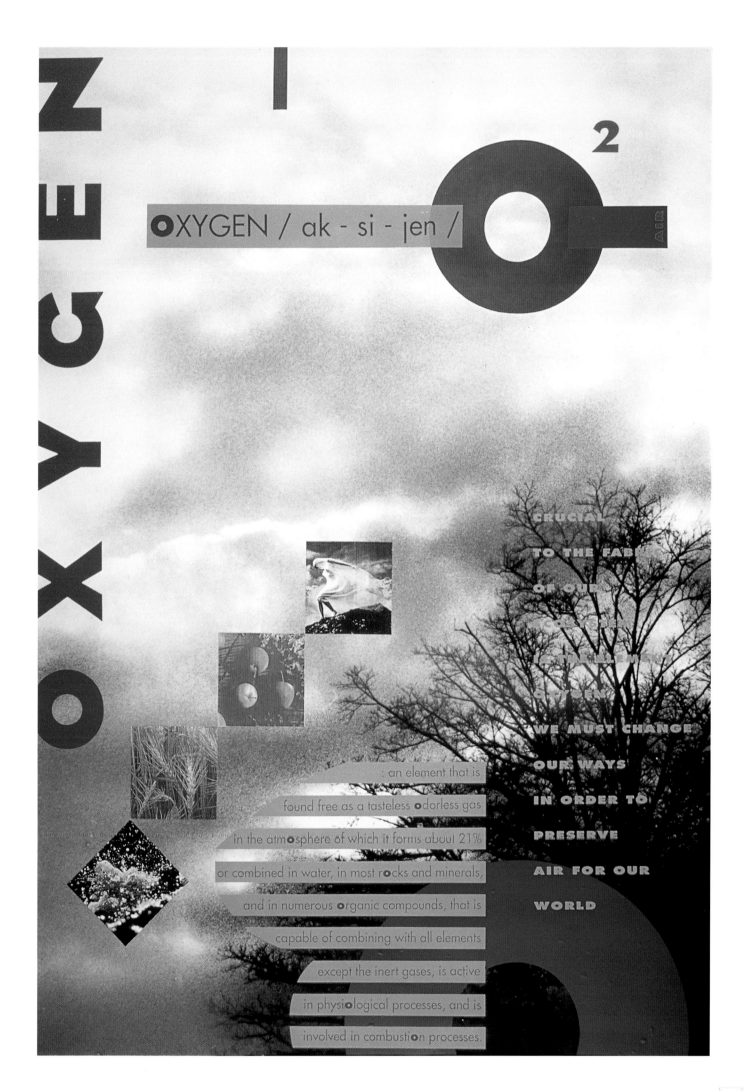

OXYGEN

O²

AIR

●XYGEN / ak - si - jen /

: an element that is

found free as a tasteless ●dorless gas

in the atm●sphere of which it forms about 21%

or combined in water, in most r●cks and minerals,

and in numerous ●rganic compounds, that is

capable of combining with all elements

except the inert gases, is active

in physi●logical processes, and is

involved in combusti●n processes.

CRUCIAL

TO THE FAB...

OF OUR

...

...

...

WE MUST CHANGE

OUR WAYS

IN ORDER TO

PRESERVE

AIR FOR OUR

WORLD

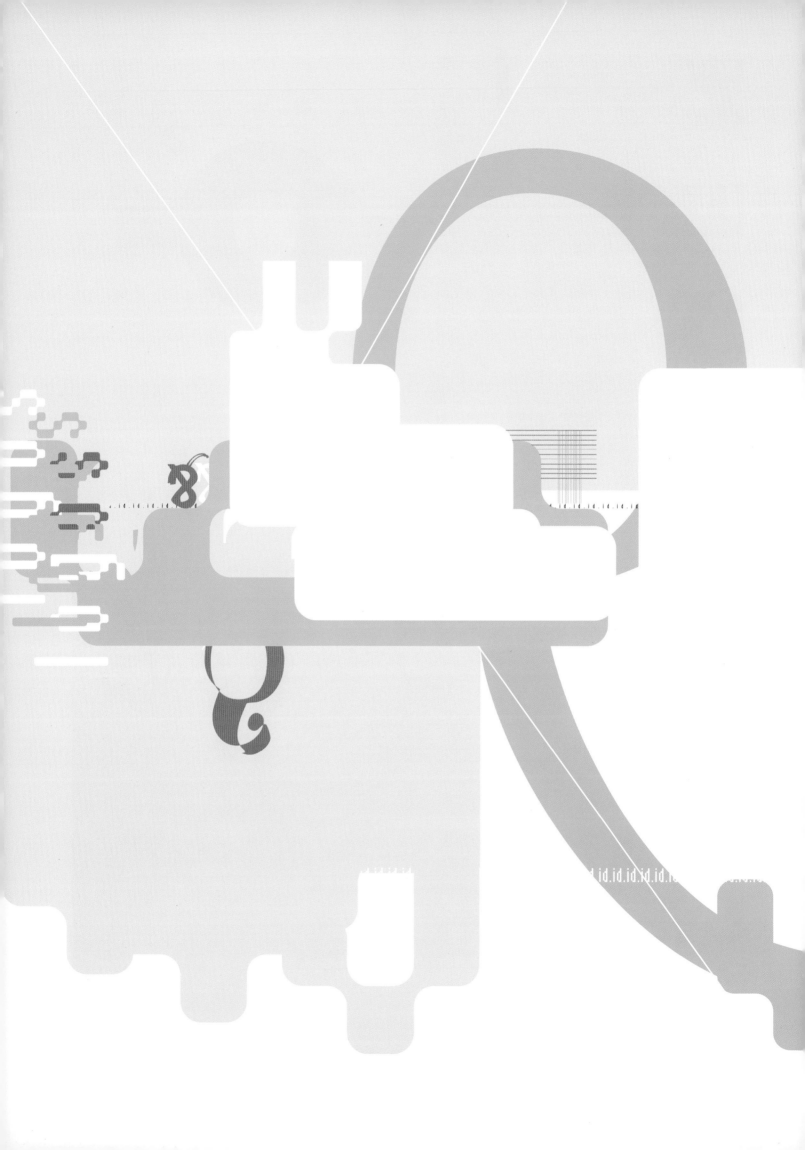

# LOGOS & corporate ids

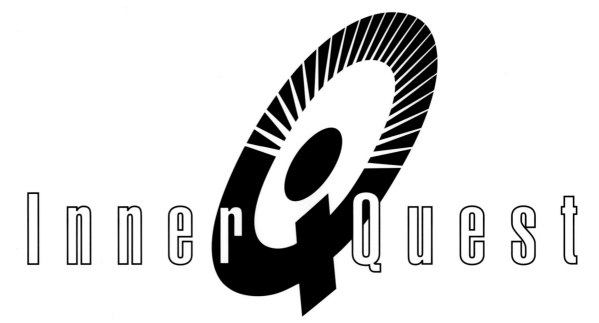

Inner Quest

DESIGN Charles E. Carpenter for Charles Carpenter Design Studio
PROJECT Inner Quest logo
CLIENT Inner Quest
TOOLS Adobe Illustrator

The designer worked with thumbnails, then on the computer. He tried a **variety of types,** which he then **converted** to paths in Illustrator. He used **distortion to make the shapes he wanted.**

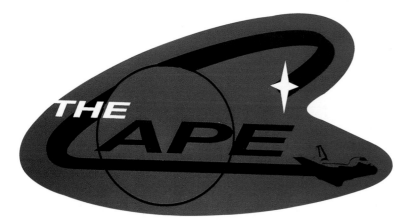

DESIGN Mike Salisbury and Mick Haggerty
for Mike Salisbury Communications, Inc.
PROJECT The Cape logo
CLIENT MTM Entertainment
TOOLS Adobe Illustrator on Macintosh

This logo was developed for a new television drama **focusing on characters involved in space programs.**

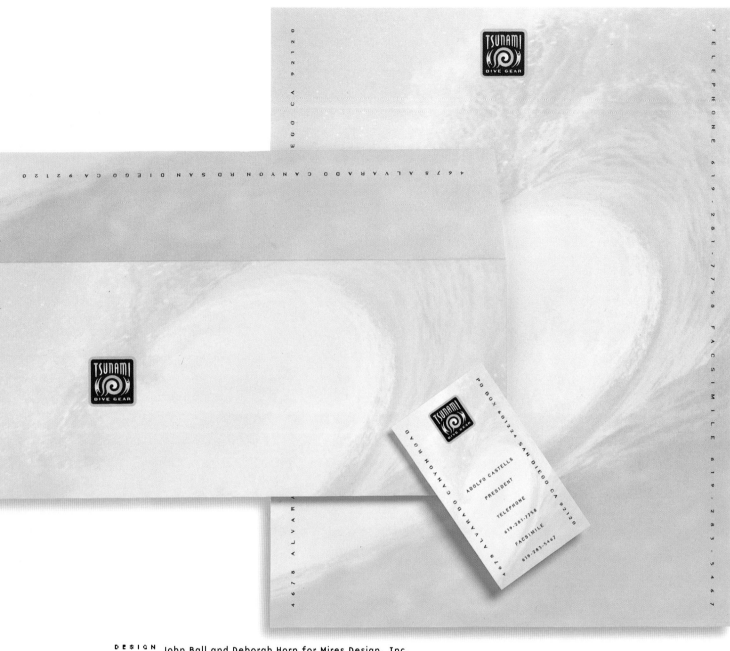

DESIGN  John Ball and Deborah Horn for Mires Design, Inc.
PROJECT  Tsunami logo
CLIENT  Tsunami Dive Gear
TOOLS  Adobe Illustrator on Macintosh

This is a **logo** for a scuba-diving product line.

DESIGN    Meighan Depke and Tony Klassen for Depke Design
PROJECT   Planet X
CLIENT    Planet X
TOOLS     Adobe Photoshop on Macintosh
FONT      Industria

This **is an illustration** of the
Planet X logo for use on business cards and stationery.

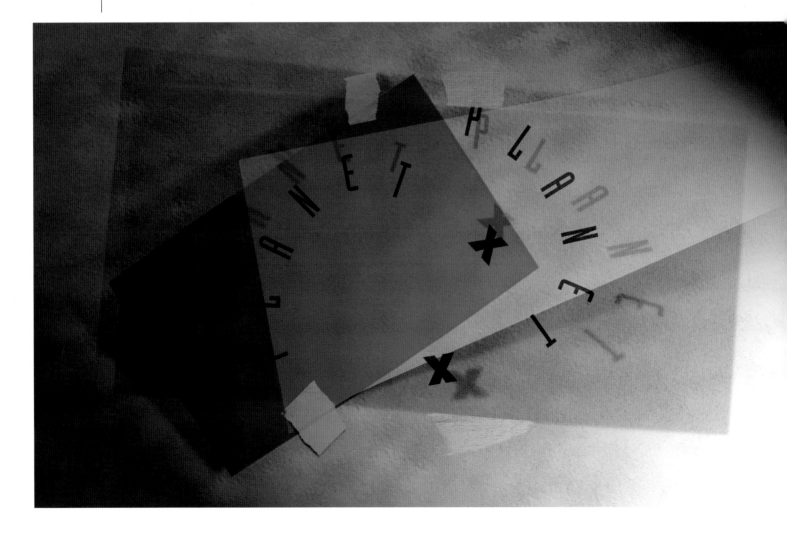

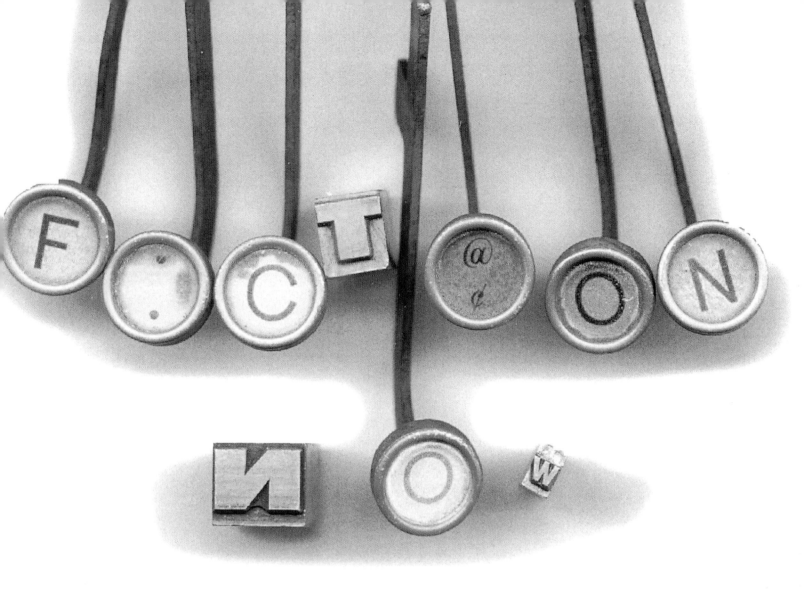

DESIGN   Mary Evelyn McGough and Mike Hand for
         Mike Salisbury Communications, Inc.
PROJECT  *Fiction Now* logo and masthead
CLIENT   Francis Ford Coppola/American Zoetrope
TOOLS    Adobe Photoshop on Macintosh
FONT     Actual old typewriter keys, Franklin Gothic

*Fiction Now* is a new writers' journal—a forum for new writers of short fiction. **Old type keys were scanned** and **manipulated to read** as a masthead.

DESIGN   Paula Menchen for PJ Graphics
PROJECT  Link
TOOLS    Adobe Illustrator on Macintosh
FONT     Borzoi Reader

This is an unrealized logo design that was **manipulated and altered** in Illustrator. The designer used Borzoi Reader and **rescaled and redrew** parts of the font.

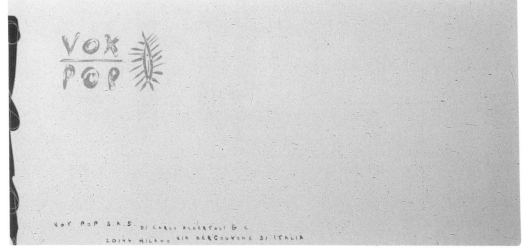

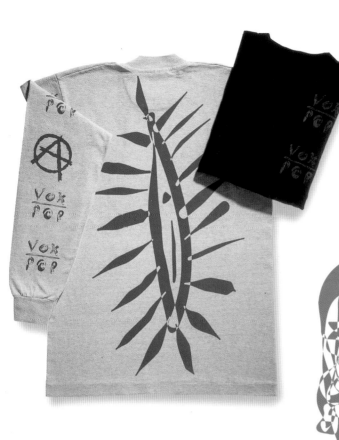

VOX
REGULAR

ABCDEFGHIJKLMNOPQ
RSTUVWXYZABCDEFGHI
JKLMNOPQRSTUVWXYZ
0123456789[\]^_`!"#$
%&'()*+,./:;<=>?@@}~※°¢
£§◦¶ß®©Trade Mark ‡…""'‚‚ß

DESIGN  Giacomo Spazio, Matteo Bologna for Matteo Bologna
Design NY/ROM Graphixxx Milano
PROJECT  Vox Pop corporate identity
CLIENT  Vox Pop
TOOLS  Fontographer, FreeHand on Macintosh
FONT  Vox (custom made)

The font and the logo were designed with a digital
tablet on FreeHand and Fontographer, **exploring the possibility** of **creating shapes with
even/odd fills.**

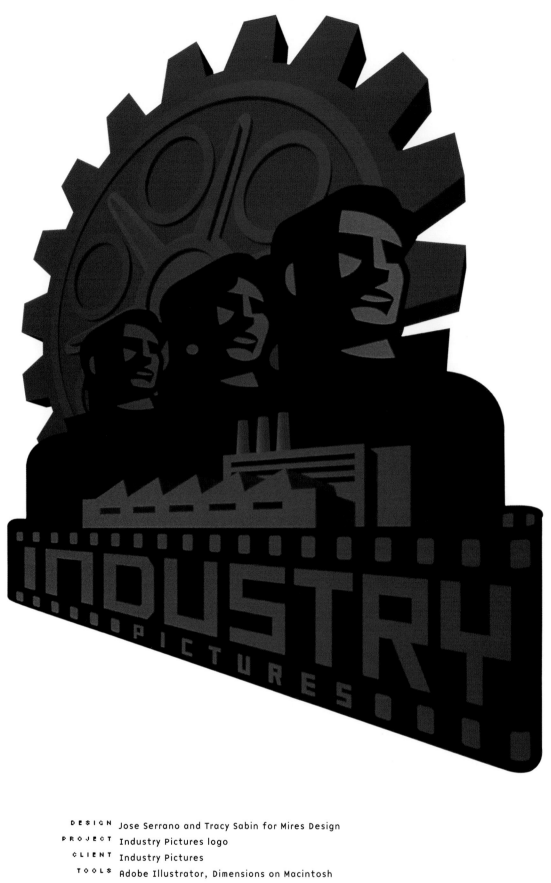

DESIGN    Jose Serrano and Tracy Sabin for Mires Design
PROJECT   Industry Pictures logo
CLIENT    Industry Pictures
TOOLS     Adobe Illustrator, Dimensions on Macintosh
FONT      Custom Font

This is the **logo** for a corporate-oriented film company.

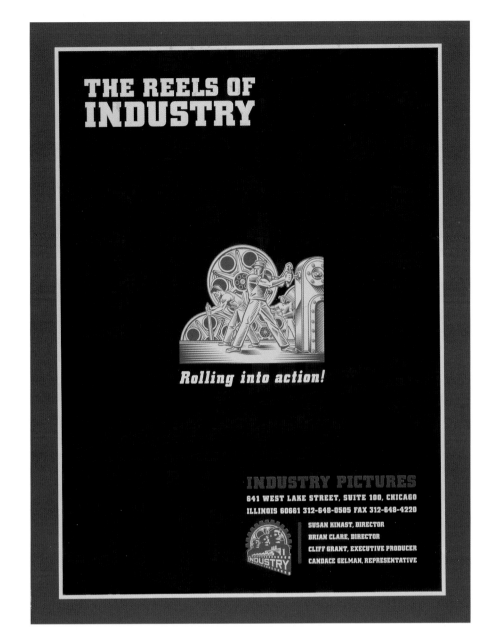

**THE REELS OF INDUSTRY**

Rolling into action!

**INDUSTRY PICTURES**
641 WEST LAKE STREET, SUITE 100, CHICAGO
ILLINOIS 60661 312-648-0505 FAX 312-648-4220

SUSAN KINAST, DIRECTOR
BRIAN CLARE, DIRECTOR
CLIFF GRANT, EXECUTIVE PRODUCER
CANDACE GELMAN, REPRESENTATIVE

D E S I G N   Kathy Carpentier-Moore and John Ball for Mires Design, Inc.
P R O J E C T   Industry Pictures logo
C L I E N T   Industry Pictures
T O O L S   Adobe Illustrator on Macintosh

The designers **wanted to capture the 1940s union worker.** The gears, factory, people, and mechanical type all come together to **convey** that feeling.

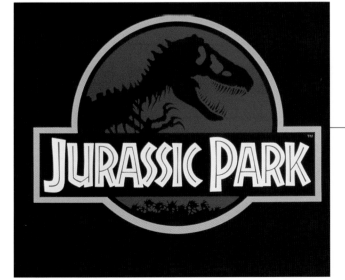

D E S I G N   Mike Salisbury for Mike Salisbury Communications, Inc.
P R O J E C T   *Jurassic Park* logo
C L I E N T   Universal Pictures
T O O L S   Adobe Illustrator on Macintosh

The type from an old sign painter's handbook was **scanned and manipulated** for this logo.

DESIGN    Fritz Klaetke for Visual Dialogue
PROJECT   Drawbridge identity
CLIENT    Drawbridge
TOOLS     QuarkXPress on Macintosh
FONTS     Avenir, Courier

The word **"Drawbridge"** metaphorically **"spans the moat"** of confusing and cryptic HTML acronyms.

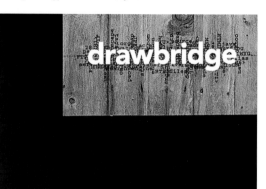

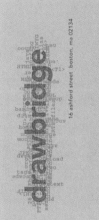

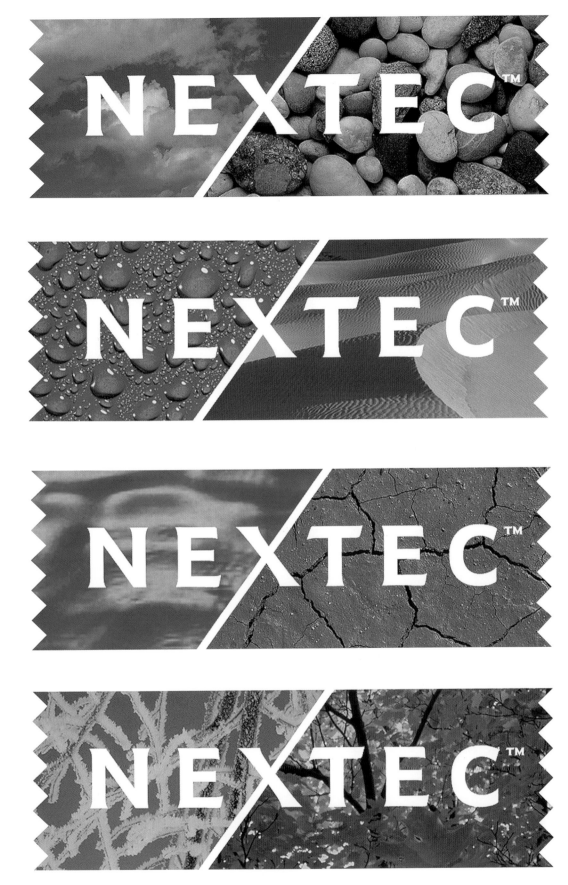

DESIGN   Kathy Carpentier-Moore and John Ball for Mires Design, Inc.
PROJECT  Nextec logos
CLIENT   Nextec Applications, Inc.
TOOLS    Adobe Illustrator, Adobe Photoshop on Macintosh

This is a logo for cold-, heat-, and moisture-resistant fabrics.

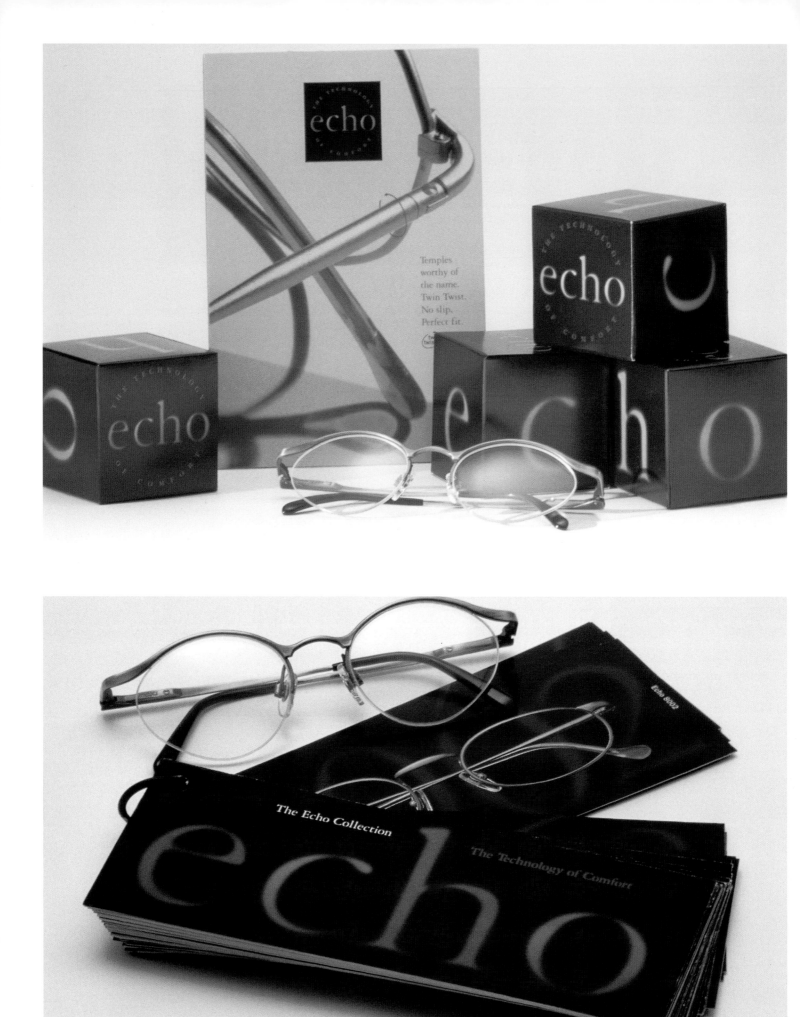

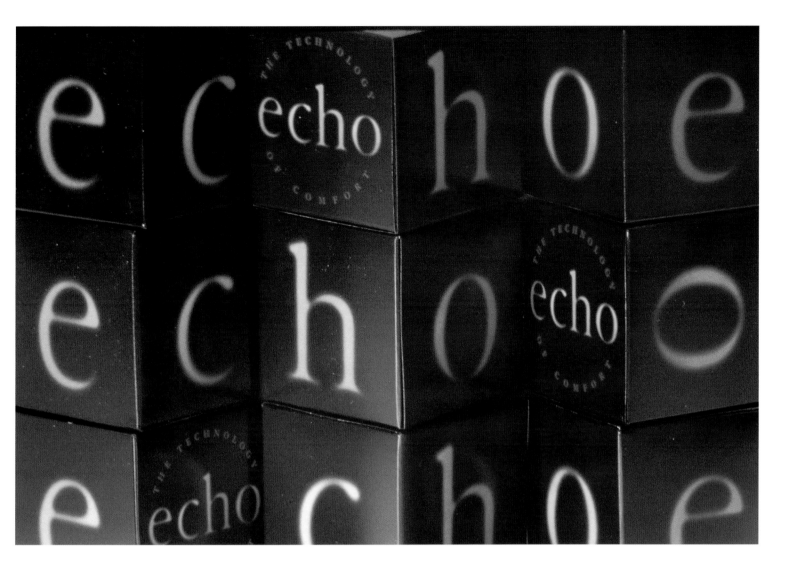

DESIGN    Michael Gericke and Sharon Harel for Pentagram Design
PROJECT   Echo Eyewear
CLIENT    Silhouette Optical
TOOLS     Adobe Illustrator, Adobe Photoshop on Macintosh
FONTS     Adobe Garamond, Univers

The identity consists of the word "echo" spelled out in **diffused type** that **subtly reverberates** against a black background, suggesting the flexible frames. The products were photographed on top of their product numbers, providing easy reference and an interesting backdrop.

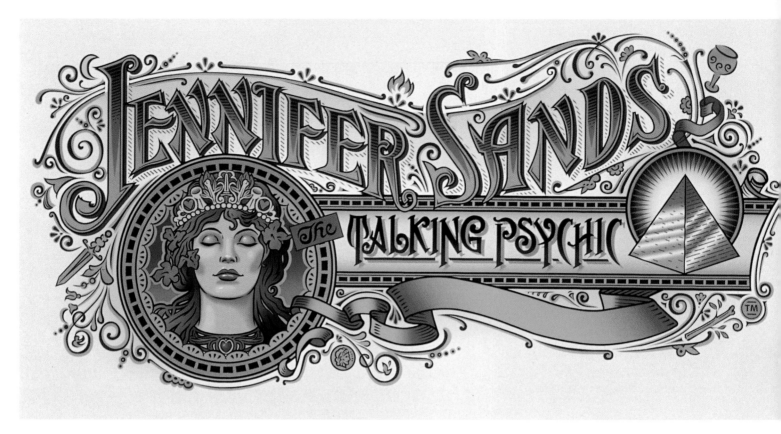

DESIGN   Jose Serrano and Tracy Sabin for Mires Design, Inc.
PROJECT  Jennifer Sands logo
CLIENT   Cranford Street
TOOLS    Adobe Illustrator on Macintosh
FONT     Custom Font

This is the **logo for a series of games** and household products.

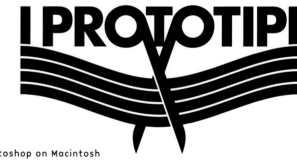

DESIGN   Gaetano Ruocco for Graphic Art Studio
PROJECT  Logo for hairdresser
CLIENT   I Prototipi
TOOLS    Adobe Illustrator, KPT Bryce, Adobe Photoshop on Macintosh
FONT     Futura Bold

The designer used Futura because he needed
**a simple linear type** for the perfect circle of the scissors.
The underline was manipulated to **resemble the wave in a hairstyle.**

# PRAVDA

## SQUEEZED

## PRAVDA
### BLACK CONDENSED

## PRAVDA
### ULTRA EXTENDED INLINE ★ ★ ★

## PRAVDA
### ULTRA EXTENDED

## PRAVDA
### ULTRA LUNGO

## PRAVDA
### HEAVY CONDENSED

## PRAVDA
### HEAVY EXTENDED

## PRAVDA
### BLACK EXTENDED

## PRAVDA
### BLACK

**DESIGN** Matteo Bologna for Matteo Bologna Design NY
**PROJECT** Pravda corporate identity
**CLIENT** Pravda
**TOOLS** Fontographer, FreeHand on Macintosh
**FONT** Pravda Family (custom made)

The project is a corporate identity for Pravda, a Russian bar in New York. The designers **designed** the font family Pravda (composed of nine different styles). This **font was used to define** the **neoconstructivist style** of the graphic identity.

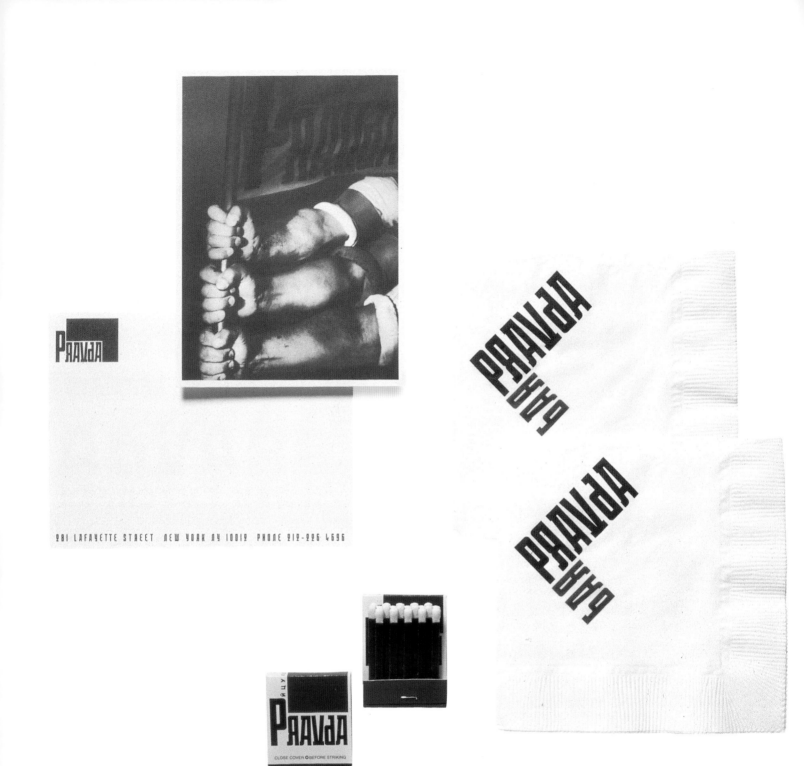

DESIGN   Matteo Bologna for Matteo Bologna Design NY
PROJECT  Pravda corporate identity
CLIENT   Pravda
TOOLS    Fontographer, FreeHand on Macintosh
FONT     Pravda Family (custom made)

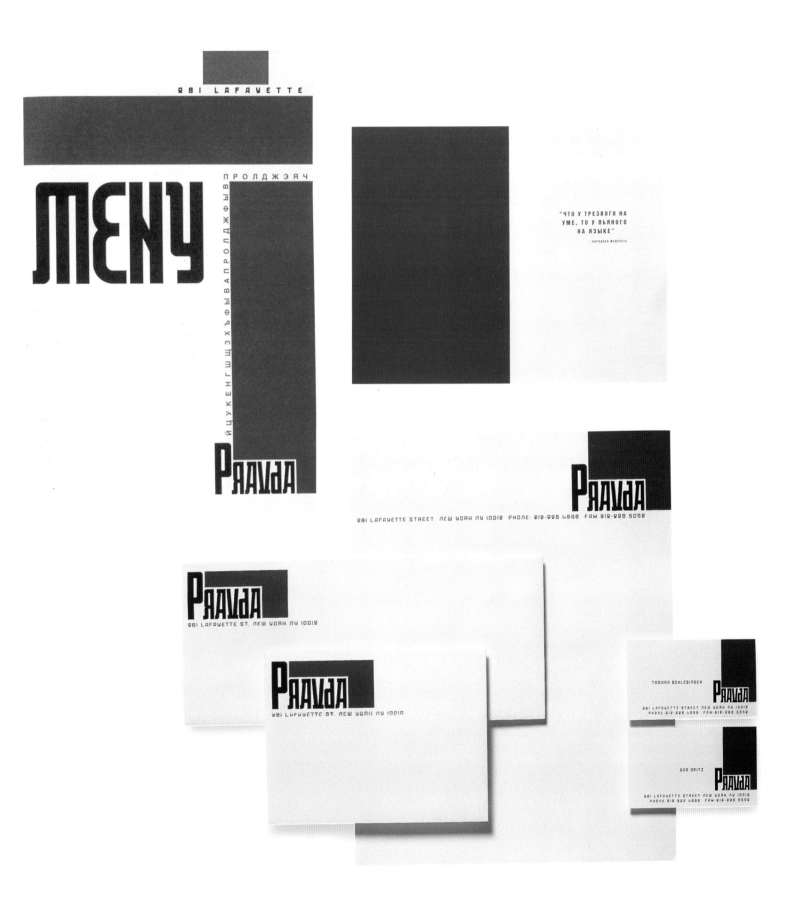

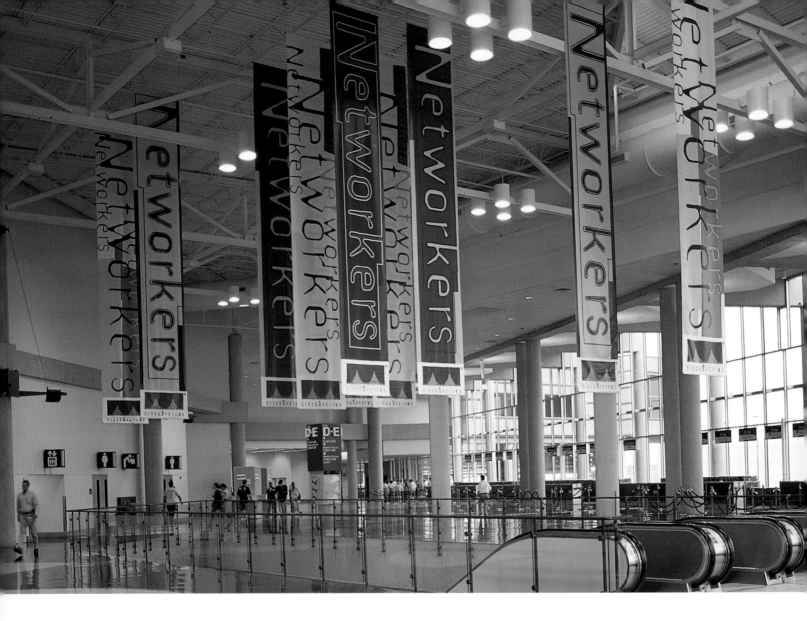

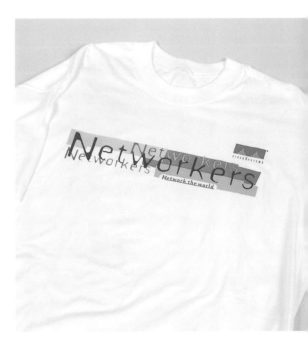

**D E S I G N**    Mark Drury for International Events
**P R O J E C T**    Networkers 1996
**C L I E N T**    Cisco Systems, Inc.
**T O O L S**    Adobe Illustrator on Macintosh
**F O N T**    Template Gothic

The font was **outlined and manipulated** in Illustrator. A rough body or inner weight **was drawn** with the Wacom tablet, giving the logo several layers.

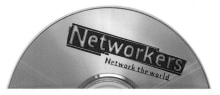

Australia
Europe
Singapore
Japan
South Africa
Latin America
USA
Canada

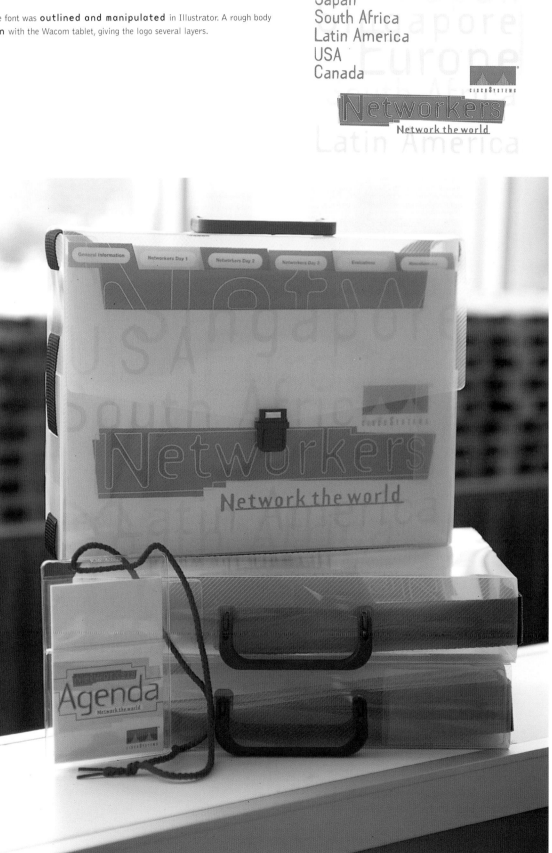

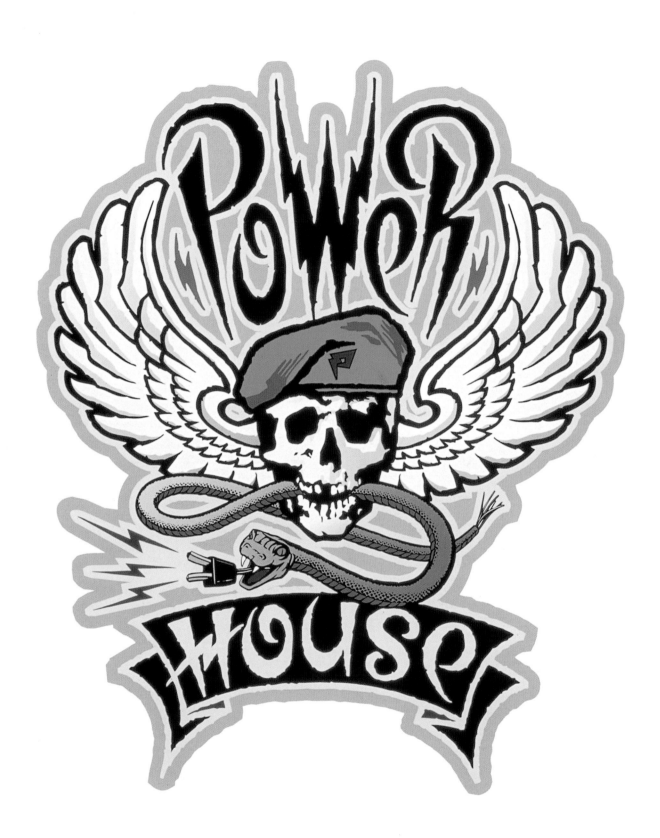

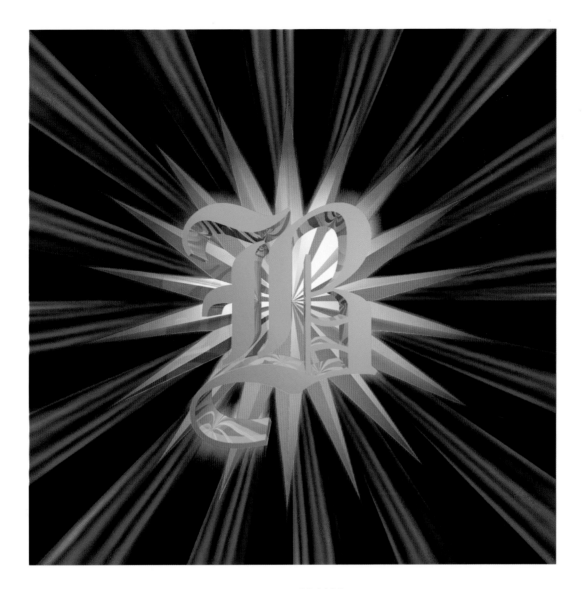

DESIGN Tony Klassen for Segura, Inc.
PROJECT B-Box
CLIENT TVT Records
TOOLS Ray Dream Designer, Adobe Photoshop on Macintosh
FONT Linoscript

This is a TVT record collection called **B-Box.**

DESIGN Mike Salisbury for Mike Salisbury Communications, Inc.
PROJECT Power House
CLIENT Stat House/Power House
TOOLS Adobe Illustrator
FONT Sketch Rough

This piece was hand **illustrated** in Adobe Illustrator. The illustrator was given a rough sketch specifying jagged, **tattoo-style type treatment.**

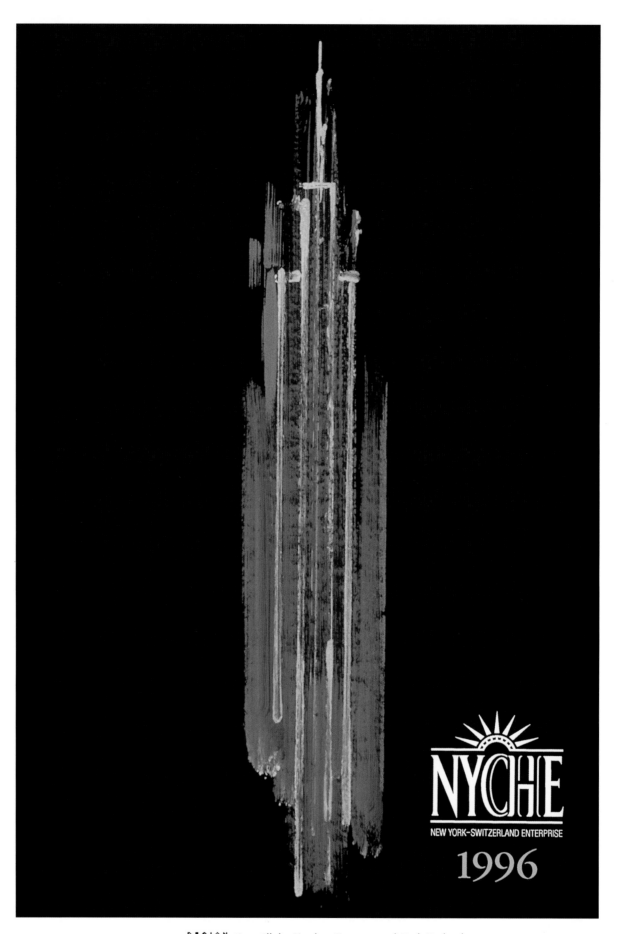

DESIGN    Hans Flink, Stephen Hooper, and Mark Krukonis
          for Hans Flink Design Inc.
PROJECT   NYCHE corporate identity
CLIENT    NYCHE Inc.
TOOLS     Adobe Illustrator on Macintosh
FONT      Arrow

This corporate logo for NYCHE represents an international agency that promotes quality business relationships between New York and Switzerland. A modified arrow font highlights the "CH" portion of the logo symbolizing Switzerland ("Confederation Helvetia"). New York is represented by the initial letters and a stylized version of the crown of liberty.

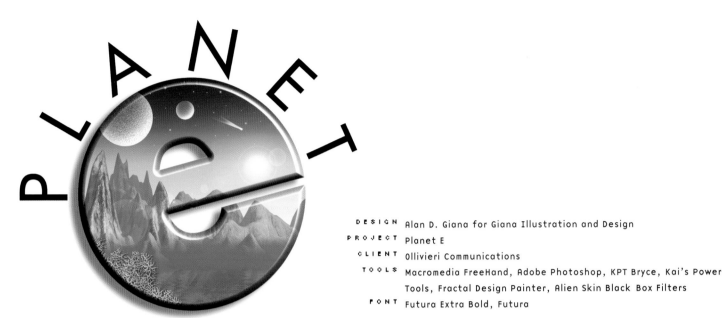

DESIGN Alan D. Giana for Giana Illustration and Design
PROJECT Planet E
CLIENT Ollivieri Communications
TOOLS Macromedia FreeHand, Adobe Photoshop, KPT Bryce, Kai's Power Tools, Fractal Design Painter, Alien Skin Black Box Filters
FONT Futura Extra Bold, Futura

The type was created in FreeHand, and then the "e" and "planet" type **were exported** individually. The designer loaded and **painted each isolated section,** created the mountain scene, and then placed them into the "e" for the final design.

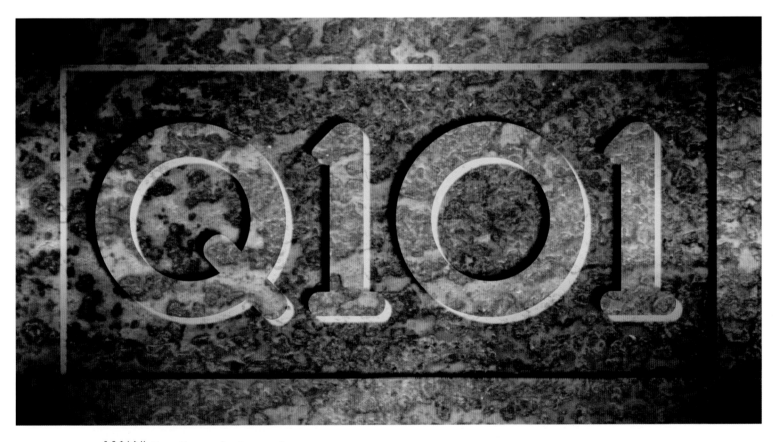

DESIGN Tony Klassen for Segura, Inc.
PROJECT Q101 logo
CLIENT Q101-Chicago radio station
TOOLS Adobe Photoshop on Macintosh

This is an **alteration** of the original logo.

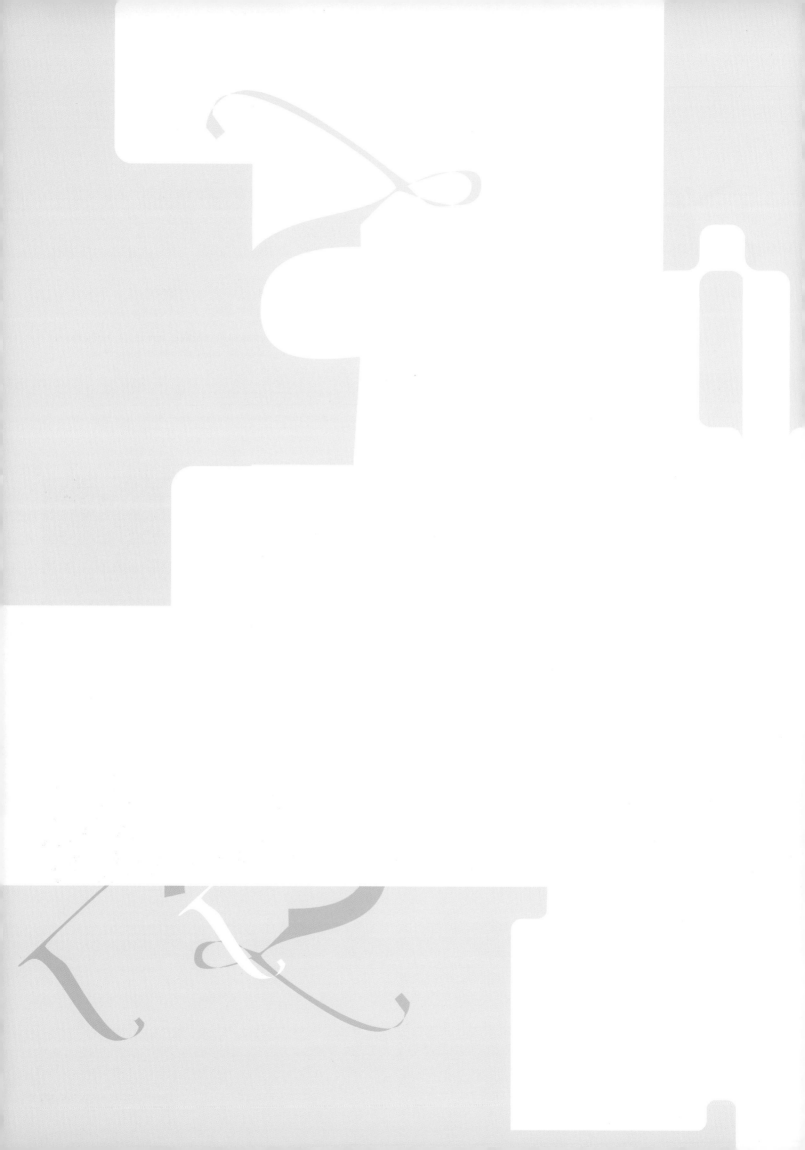

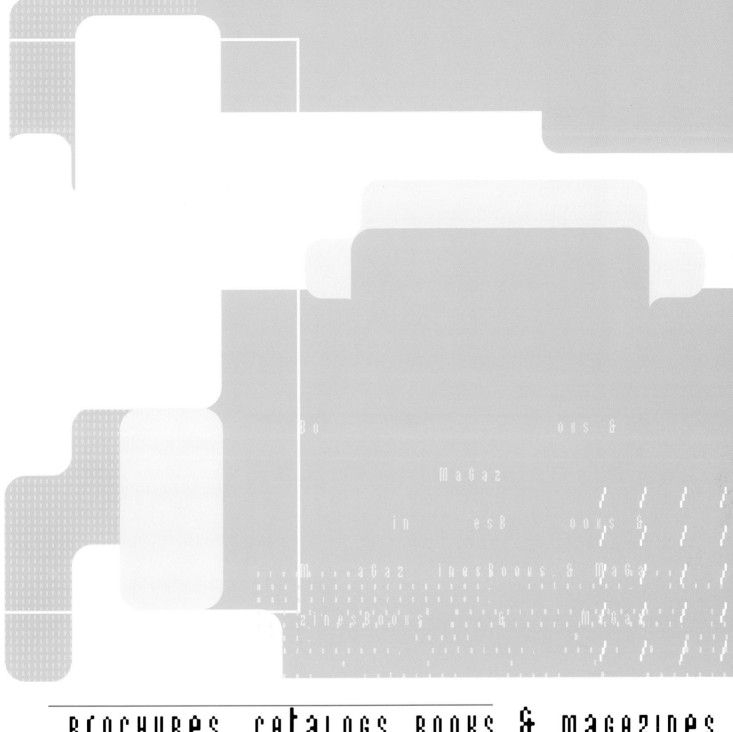

# BROCHURES, CATALOGS, BOOKS & MAGAZINES

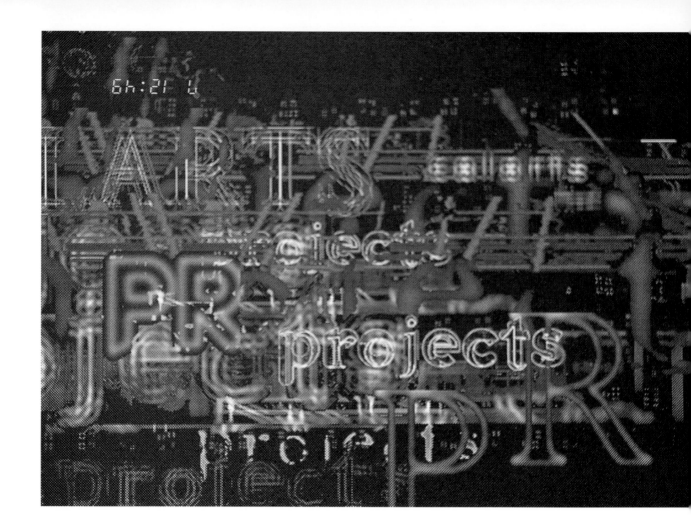

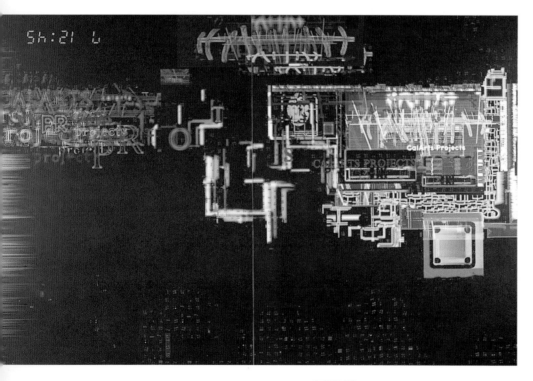

DESIGN   Deborah Littlejohn and Shawn McKinney
PROJECT  *Fast Forward* catalog spread
CLIENT   California Institute of the Arts
TOOLS    Adobe Photoshop
FONTS    Perpetua, Vag Rounded, Keedy Sans

This catalog, designed by CalArts graduate students,
presented **a series of lectures and workshops** with guest designers
that explored the **potential of the computer in design.**
It uses every known Photoshop filter available in 1993 **multiplied by 1,000 times.**

DESIGN     Mary Evelyn McGough and Mike Salisbury for Mike Salisbury Communications, Inc.
PROJECT     *Rage* brochure and box press kit
CLIENT     *Rage* magazine
TOOLS     Adobe Illustrator, QuarkXPress on Macintosh
FONTS     Platelet, Compacta, Orator

This is **a press kit to announce** a new men's magazine targeted at younger readers. Type was overlapped, stretched, and shadowed to give **a dense, busy look.**

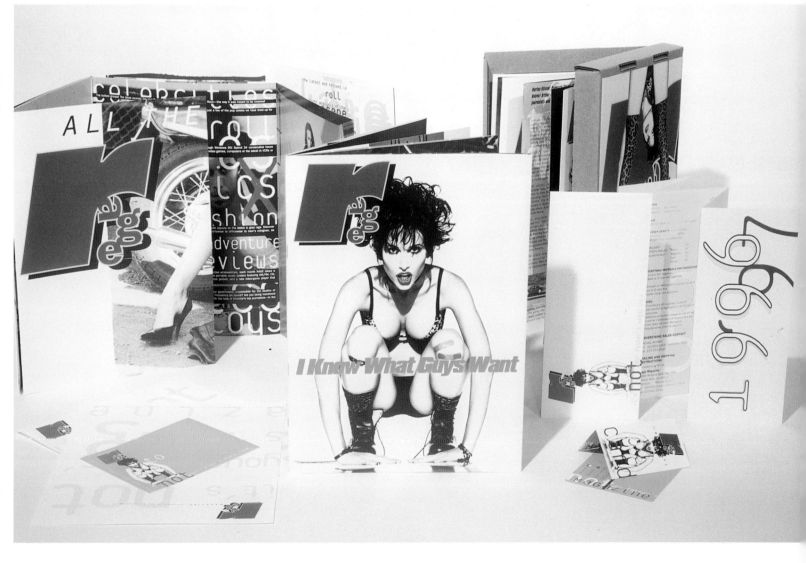

**DESIGN** Jose A. Serrano for Mires Design, Inc.
**PROJECT** *Total Racquetball* 1993
**CLIENT** Ektelon
**TOOLS** Adobe Illustrator, Adobe Photoshop on Macintosh

*Total Racquetball* **is an annual publication** that features the client's entire line
of products, articles, tips on nutrition and on how to improve
one's game, **interviews with pros**, and so on.
The type was selected because it conveyed a **sportslike attitude.**

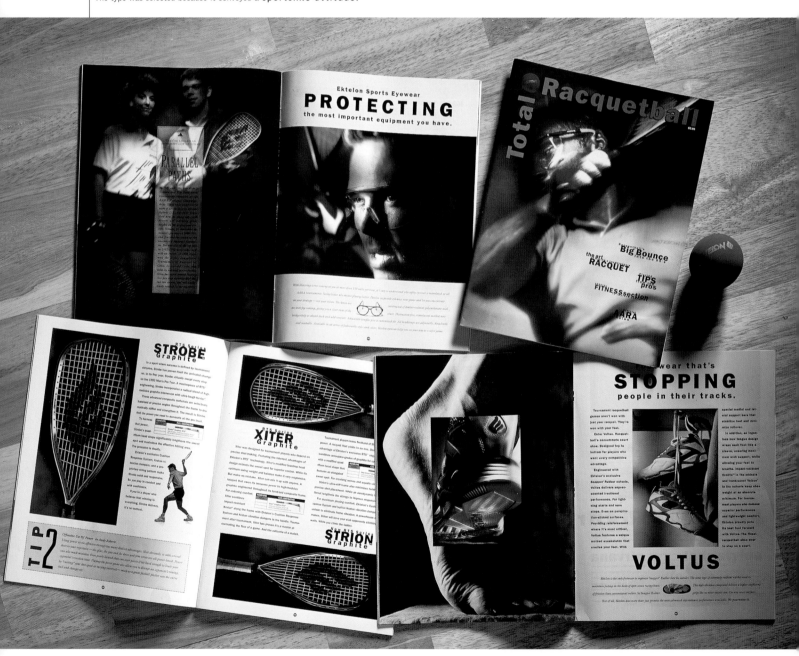

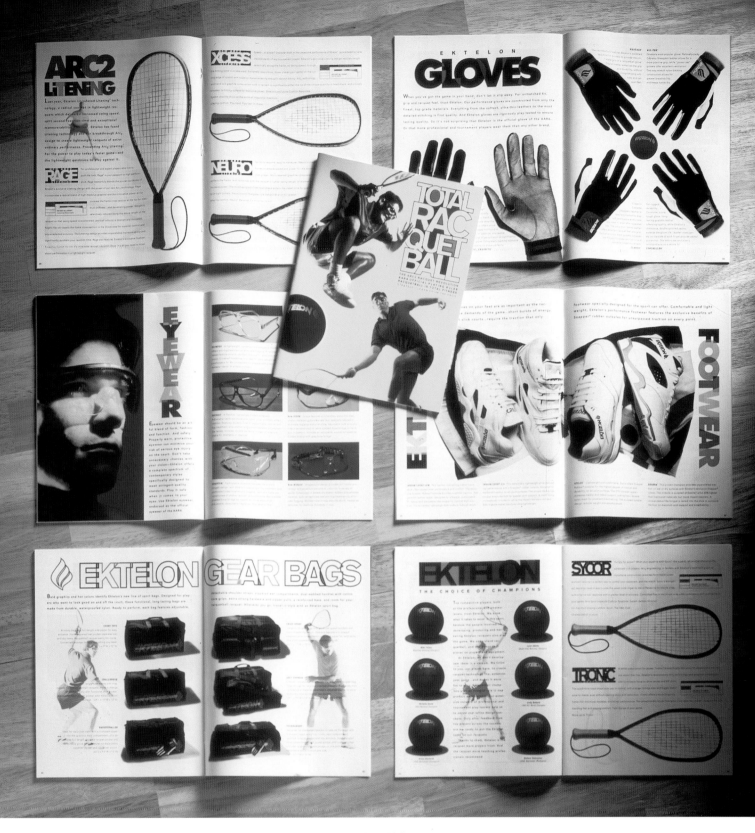

DESIGN Jose A. Serrano for Mires Design, Inc.
PROJECT *Total Racquetball 1994*
CLIENT Ektelon
TOOLS Adobe Illustrator, Adobe Photoshop on Macintosh

*Total Racquetball* is an annual publication that features **the client's entire line of products,** articles, tips on nutrition and on how to **improve one's game**, interviews with pros, and so on. The type was selected because it conveyed a **sportslike attitude.**

Almost as if everyone from the neighborhood will keep you **hot, piles of stuff together.**, an enormous portfolio of photographs, drawings, words, ink, and I couldn't even think of a quote (I think it was during this sequence of photos huge vile classics that things began to get difficult, it's hard to know)

**it's hard to know the origin of THINGS.**

we would remember where those wings will fly you, for it's our secret, a child's hidden language, a history of heavenly music, of one together, of other things into songs in one voice, in another from its customary, and we could of course just retell the story in our own way, how a watcher loses himself, dissolves among shadows patching together into one lengthened out shape, a mirror of a former GATHERING. ALL OTHER WORKS. ALL OTHER HANDS . in mysterious

EXACTITUDE, spattered closeness.

**for everything is JUST BEGINNING.**

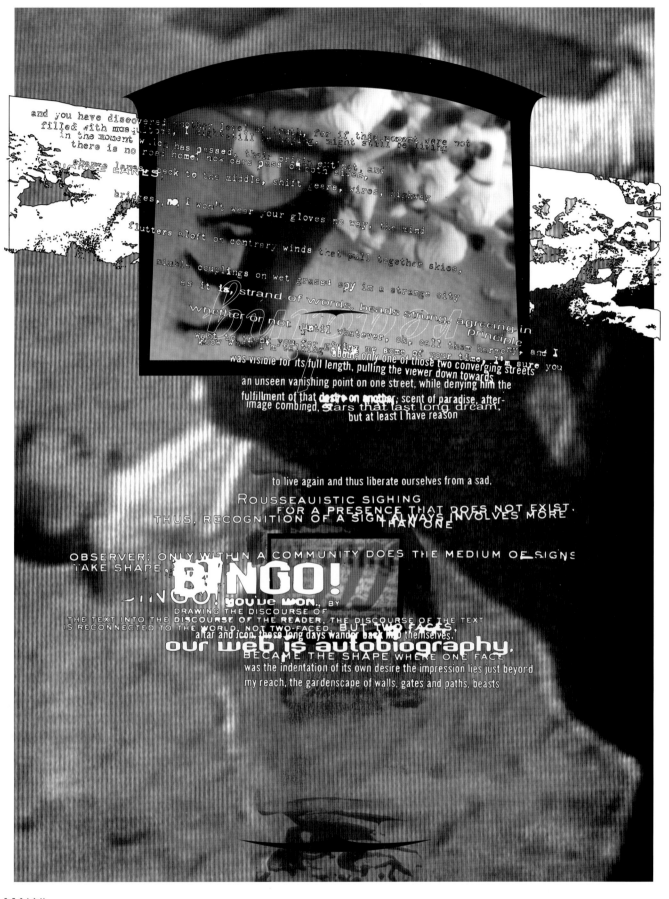

DESIGN    Stephen Farrell for SLIP
PROJECT   A House Swarming!
CLIENT    *Private Arts* literary/arts journal
TOOLS     Adobe Illustrator, Adobe Photoshop, Adobe Streamline on Macintosh
FONTS     Beach Savage, Evangelic, Escalido, Werkman-Round,
          Atsackers Gothic, Coronet, 1940 Smith Corona Typewriter Elite

"A House Swarming!" was published as a **poem/foreword** in
the literary/art journal *Private Arts*.
The design **fractures** both the **letterforms** and narrative of a text,
which is composed of bits plagiarized from other texts in the journal.

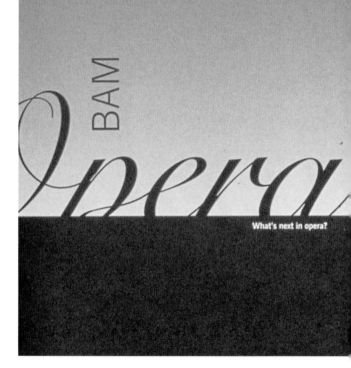

BAM

*Opera*

What's next in opera?

DESIGN   Michael Bierut and Emily Hayes for Pentagram Design
PROJECT   Brooklyn Academy of Music opera brochure
CLIENT   Brooklyn Academy of Music
TOOLS   QuarkXPress on Macintosh
FONT   Snell Roundhand

The wide stripes partially **conceal the type** to suggest something coming over the horizon,
**a visual metaphor** for the Festival's focus on emerging talent.
Subsequent brochures use **variations on this theme,**
**incorporating script** or simply cutting off lower parts of letters.

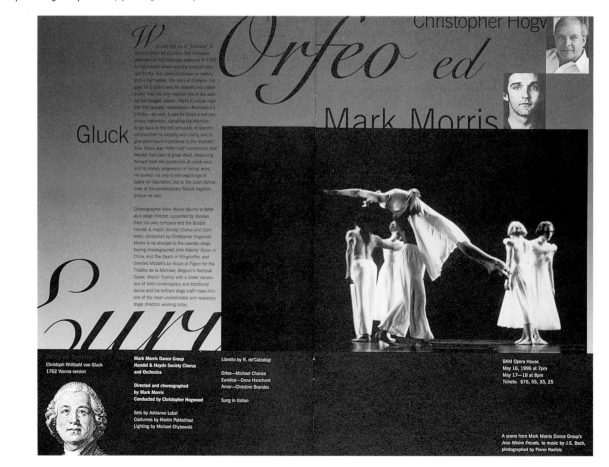

*Orfeo ed*

Christopher Hogw

Mark Morris

Gluck

Christoph Willibald von Gluck
1762 Vienna version

Mark Morris Dance Group
Handel & Haydn Society Chorus
and Orchestra

Directed and choreographed
by Mark Morris
Conducted by Christopher Hogwood

Sets by Adrianne Lobel
Costumes by Martin Pakledinaz
Lighting by Michael Chybowski

Libretto by R. de'Calzabigi

Orfeo—Michael Chance
Euridice—Dana Hanchard
Amor—Christine Brandes

Sung in Italian

BAM Opera House
May 16, 1996 at 7pm
May 17—18 at 8pm
Tickets:  $75, 55, 35, 25

A scene from Mark Morris Dance Group's
*Jesu Meine Freude*, to music by J.S. Bach,
photographed by Pierre Radisic

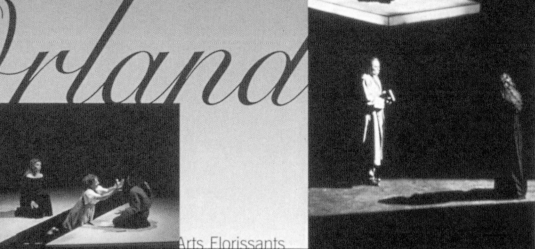

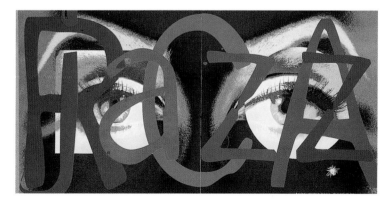

DESIGN Norman Moore for Design Art, Inc.
PROJECT  RCA Jazz catalog
CLIENT   RCA/BMG
TOOLS    Adobe Photoshop, QuarkXPress on Macintosh
FONT     Degenerate

This is a *jazz* catalog cover.

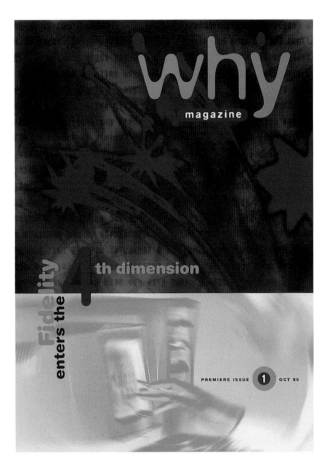

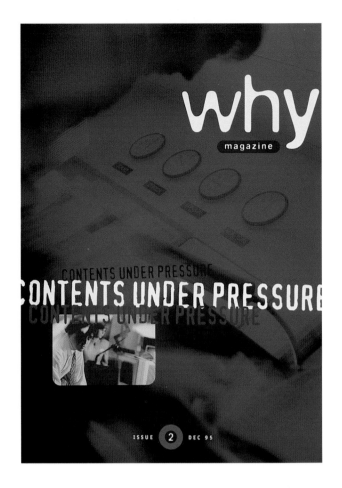

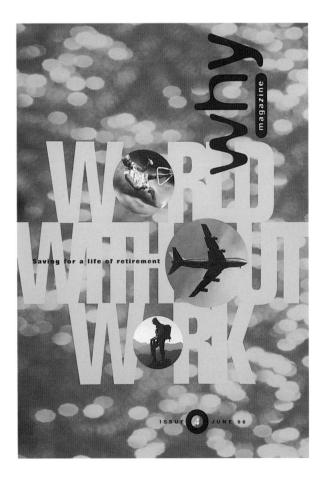

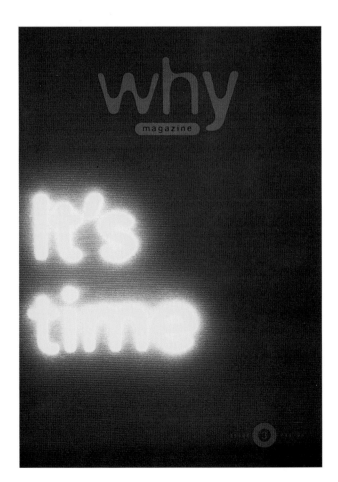

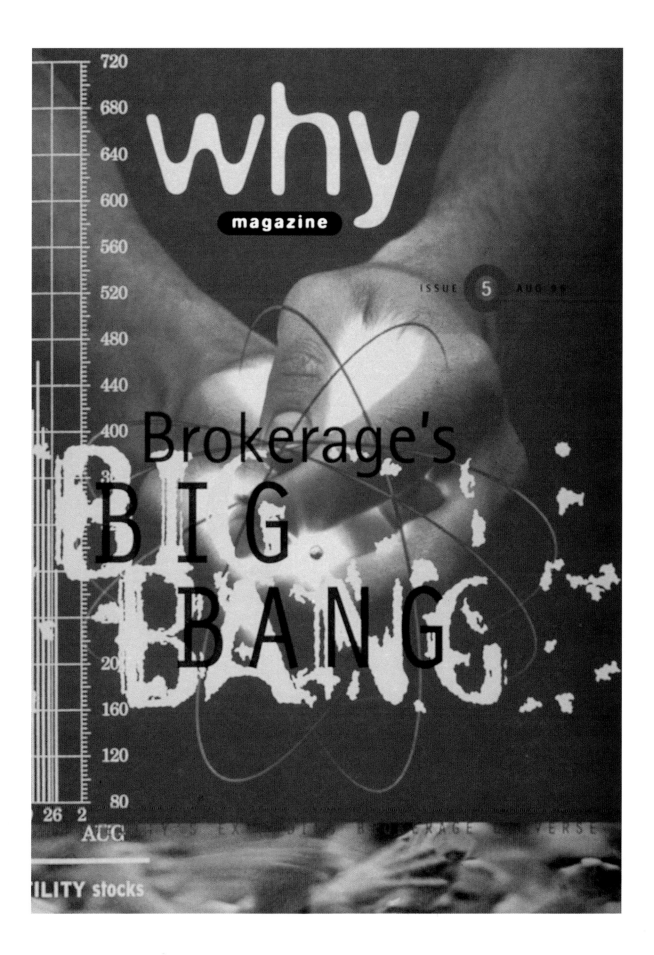

DESIGN Clifford Stoltze and Dina Radeka for Stoltze Design
PROJECT *Why Magazine*, issues 1-5
CLIENT Fidelity Investments

*Why Magazine* is an internal publication of Fidelity Retail Communications.
It provides context for **key Fidelity strategies and businesses.**

Ronald C. Hill

T R A N S P O R T A T I O N

RONALD C. HILL
FORD CHAIR, TRANSPORTATION DESIGN DEPARTMENT

"The transportation design profession is undergoing tremendous change. At Art Center we look for those students who question the status quo, the ones who are convinced that they can design a better, more *attractive, and more efficient* vehicle. Our students come to us with that drive and creative urge, but it's our task to provide the methodologies and tools to allow them to achieve their full potential. Transportation design is particularly challenging because of its enormous impact on our society. Future designers who respond sensitively to these challenges will provide inestimable benefit to the environment."

TRANSPORTATION DESIGN

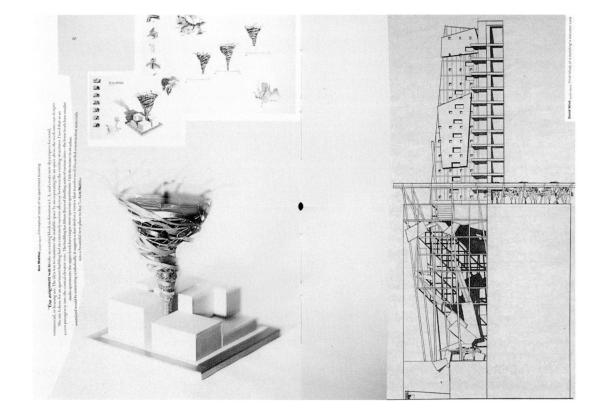

**Ken Mattias** 1997 term. *Conceptual study of an apartment building*

"Our assignment was to take an existing block in downtown L.A. and create new skyscrapers for retail, commercial, or housing use. The site was to maximize the available space by incorporating the air space above the work into your design. The site I chose for an apartment building had an extremely narrow alleyway between the existing structures I used that as an access passageway into the ground-level core. The building has fifteen floors of dwelling units of various sizes—the lower levels have smaller studio apartments, the upper levels have larger, more spacious apartments. I felt the twister in an urban wasteland would be interesting symbolically; it suggests a short-lived or a vortex that transform used discarded construction materials into a beautiful new place to live." —**Ken Mattias**

**David Wick** 1997 term. *Final study of a building's structure core*

**DESIGN** Art Center Design Office

**PROJECT** Recruitment Catalog for Art Center College of Design, 1995-96

**CLIENT** Art Center College of Design

**TOOLS** QuarkXPress, Adobe Illustrator, Adobe Photoshop

**FONTS** Lip Normal, Tema Cantante, Perpetua, Minion

The perforation bisects the headlines identifying the areas of study at Art Center, creating **hybrid words** and opening our minds to the interdisciplinary and multidisciplinary environment at the college. The typography momentarily forgets its classical roots and its autonomy. **Certain elements** of the typography were **randomly "distressed"** so that its fluidity is revealed as it is affected by surrounding elements.

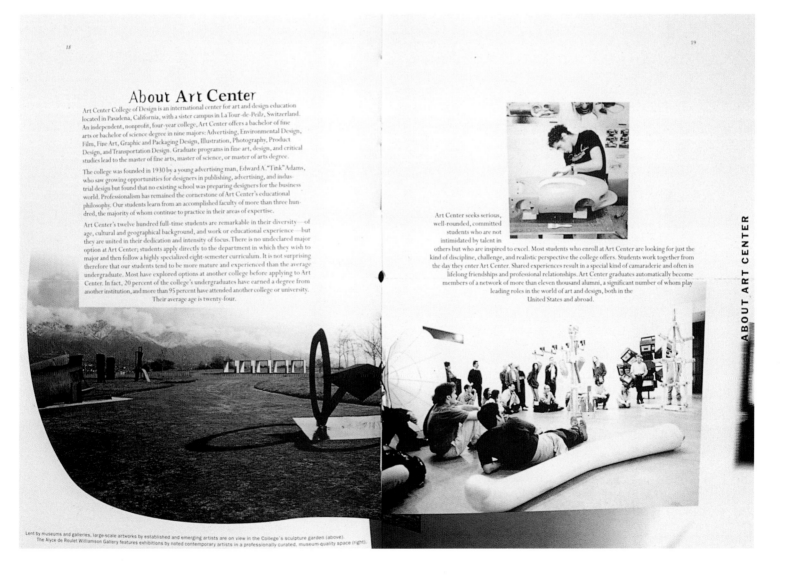

## About Art Center

Art Center College of Design is an international center for art and design education located in Pasadena, California, with a sister campus in La Tour-de-Peilz, Switzerland. An independent, nonprofit, four-year college, Art Center offers a bachelor of fine arts or bachelor of science degree in nine majors: Advertising, Environmental Design, Film, Fine Art, Graphic and Packaging Design, Illustration, Photography, Product Design, and Transportation Design. Graduate programs in fine art, design, and critical studies lead to the master of fine arts, master of science, or master of arts degree.

The college was founded in 1930 by a young advertising man, Edward A. "Tink" Adams, who saw growing opportunities for designers in publishing, advertising, and industrial design but found that no existing school was preparing designers for the business world. Professionalism has remained the cornerstone of Art Center's educational philosophy. Our students learn from an accomplished faculty of more than three hundred, the majority of whom continue to practice in their areas of expertise.

Art Center's twelve hundred full-time students are remarkable in their diversity—of age, cultural and geographical background, and work or educational experience—but they are united in their dedication and intensity of focus. There is no undeclared major option at Art Center; students apply directly to the department in which they wish to major and then follow a highly specialized eight-semester curriculum. It is not surprising therefore that our students tend to be more mature and experienced than the average undergraduate. Most have explored options at another college before applying to Art Center. In fact, 20 percent of the college's undergraduates have earned a degree from another institution, and more than 95 percent have attended another college or university. Their average age is twenty-four.

Art Center seeks serious, well-rounded, committed students who are not intimidated by talent in others but who are inspired to excel. Most students who enroll at Art Center are looking for just the kind of discipline, challenge, and realistic perspective the college offers. Students work together from the day they enter Art Center. Shared experiences result in a special kind of camaraderie and often in lifelong friendships and professional relationships. Art Center graduates automatically become members of a network of more than eleven thousand alumni, a significant number of whom play leading roles in the world of art and design, both in the United States and abroad.

Lent by museums and galleries, large-scale artworks by established and emerging artists are on view in the College's sculpture garden (above). The Alyce de Roulet Williamson Gallery features exhibitions by noted contemporary artists in a professionally curated, museum-quality space (right).

**ABOUT ART CENTER**

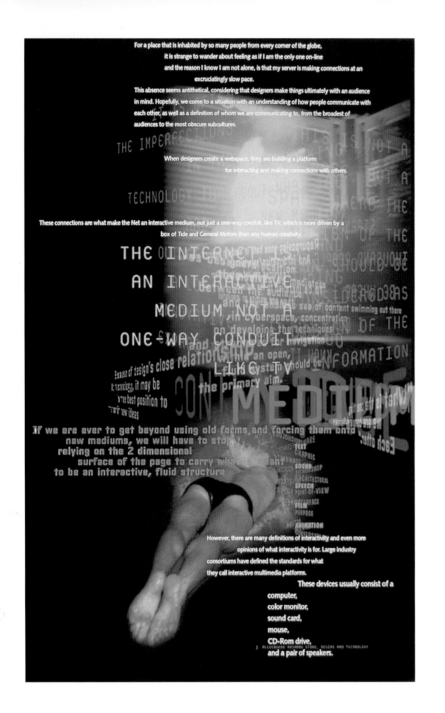

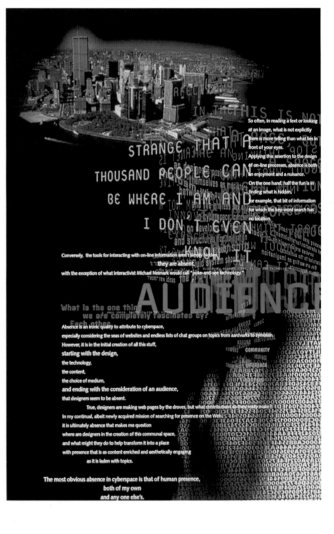

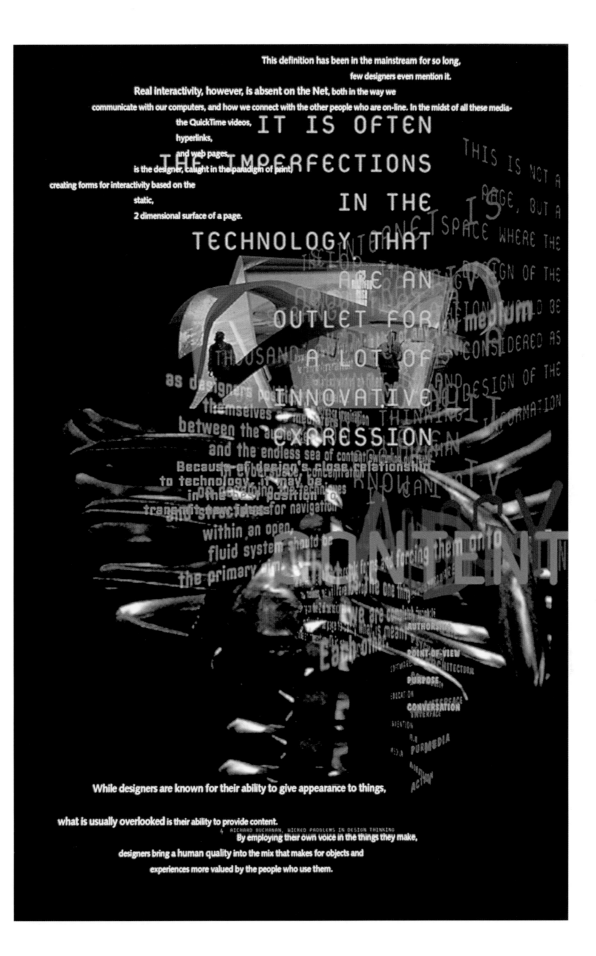

**DESIGN** Deborah Littlejohn
**PROJECT** Article on webspace design
**TOOLS** Photoshop on Macintosh
**FONTS** Platelet, Hobo, Clicker

These panels demonstrate **3-dimensional text** as applied to the Internet. Photoshop was used to mimic a proposed **inhabitable space** in which the **audience can communicate** in a 3-dimensional world.

# PAPER

THE BIG FLIRT

## Patricia Arquette

Wooing John Woo • Spanish *Fly* Pedro Almodóvar
Spike Lee's Phone-Sex Girl
MUSIC: Lovin' DJ Krush, *Maxwell*, The Supreme Dicks

DESIGN    Malcolm Turk and Bridget De Socio for Malcolm Turk Studios
PROJECT   *Paper* magazine cover, March 1996
CLIENT    *Paper* magazine
TOOLS     Adobe Illustrator, Adobe Photoshop on Macintosh
FONT      Futura Extra Bold

The logo was **created with channel offsets,** embossing,
lighting effects, and layer masks. **The smoke was photographed** against a black background
and **scanned** before being manipulated to create a cleaner image.

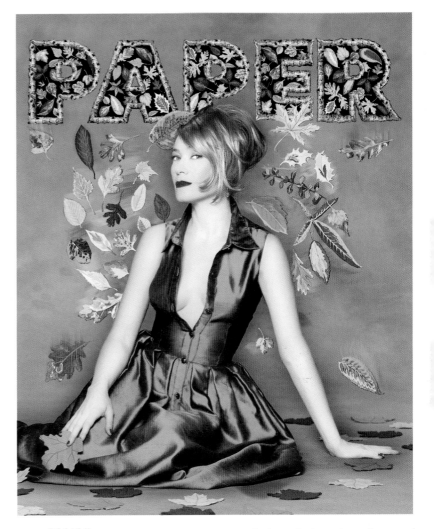

DESIGN    Malcolm Turk and Bridget De Socio for Malcolm Turk Studios
PROJECT   *Paper* magazine cover, June 1996
CLIENT    *Paper* magazine
TOOLS     Adobe Illustrator, Adobe Photoshop on Macintosh
FONT      Futura Extra Bold

**Water droplets** were photographed on a blue screen
to allow for ease in composition. **The logo's cutout appearance**
was accomplished through shadowing and layering.
**An embossed stroke** was then added to give the logo more definition.

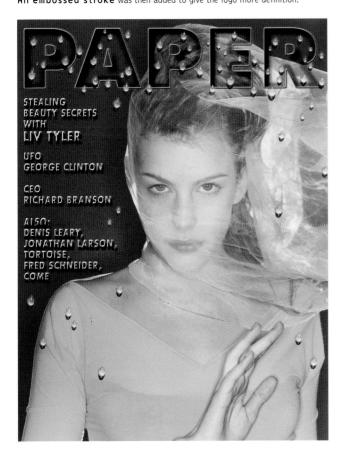

DESIGN    Malcolm Turk and Bridget De Socio for Malcolm Turk Studios
PROJECT   *Paper* magazine cover, November 1995
CLIENT    *Paper* magazine
TOOLS     Adobe Illustrator, Adobe Photoshop on Macintosh
FONT      Futura Extra Bold

Both the leaves and the type border were scanned
and then manipulated.

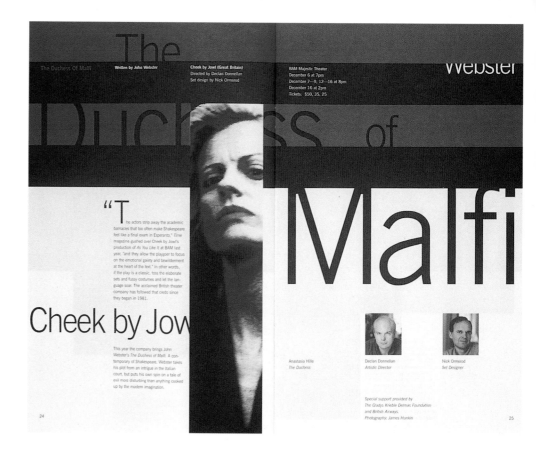

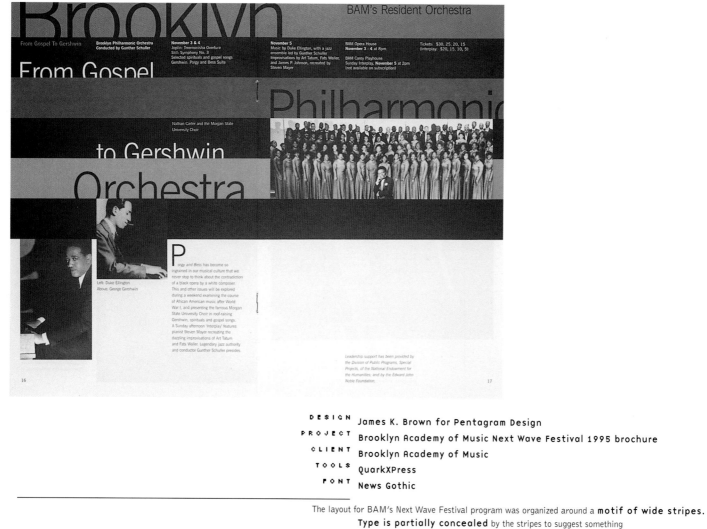

DESIGN    James K. Brown for Pentagram Design
PROJECT   Brooklyn Academy of Music Next Wave Festival 1995 brochure
CLIENT    Brooklyn Academy of Music
TOOLS     QuarkXPress
FONT      News Gothic

The layout for BAM's Next Wave Festival program was organized around a **motif of wide stripes.**
**Type is partially concealed** by the stripes to suggest something
"coming over the horizon," a visual metaphor for the **festival's focus on emerging talent.**
Subsequent brochures use different variations,
incorporating script or simply **cutting off lower parts of letters.**

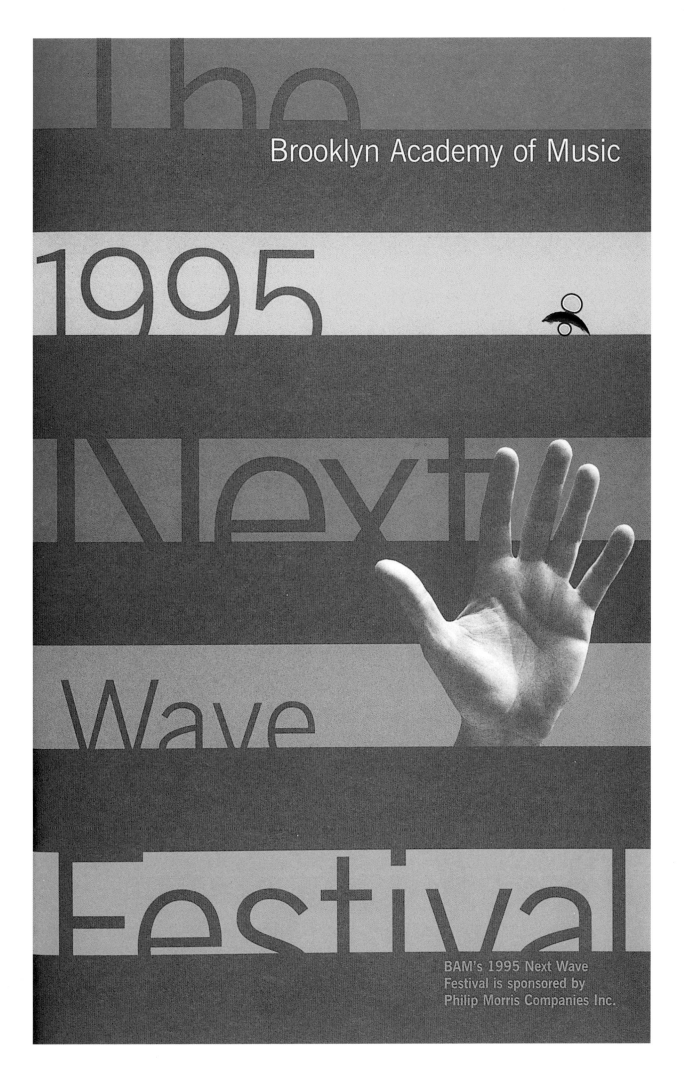

The
1995
Next
Wave
Festival

Brooklyn Academy of Music

BAM's 1995 Next Wave
Festival is sponsored by
Philip Morris Companies Inc.

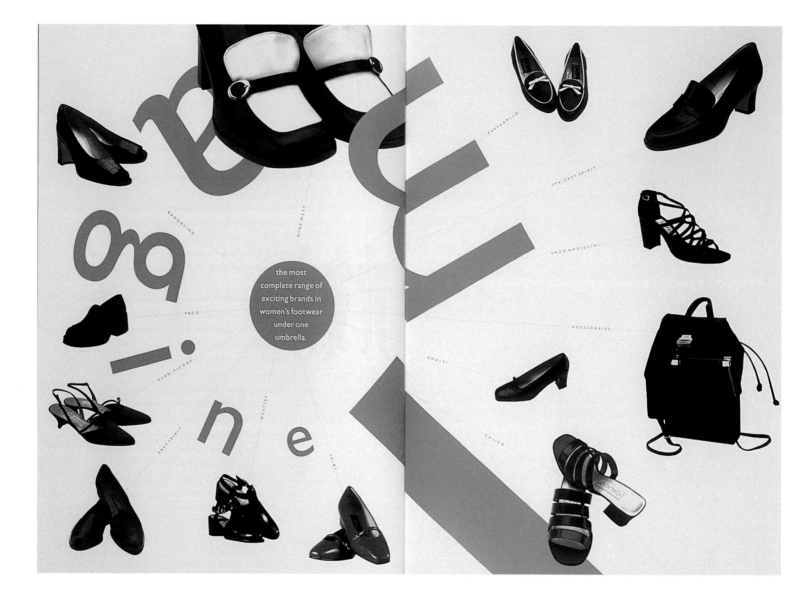

the most complete range of exciting brands in women's footwear under one umbrella.

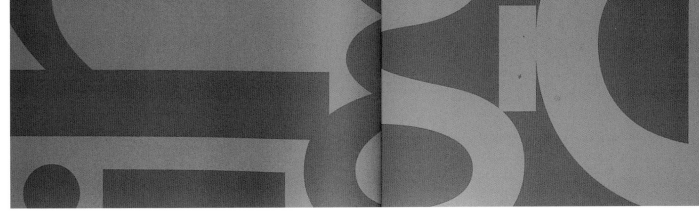

Imagine the capacity to do it, do it right, and do it right now.

DESIGN   James K. Brown for Pentagram Design
PROJECT  Nine West 1995 annual report
CLIENT   Nine West Group, Inc.
TOOLS    Adobe Illustrator, QuarkXPress on Macintosh
FONTS    Gill Sans

Nine West Group is **a leading designer**, developer,
and marketer of women's fashion footwear. The cover presents an image that is focused **toward the future.**
**Bold and imaginative typographic treatments** emphasize the company's
success in understanding and meeting the needs of its customers.

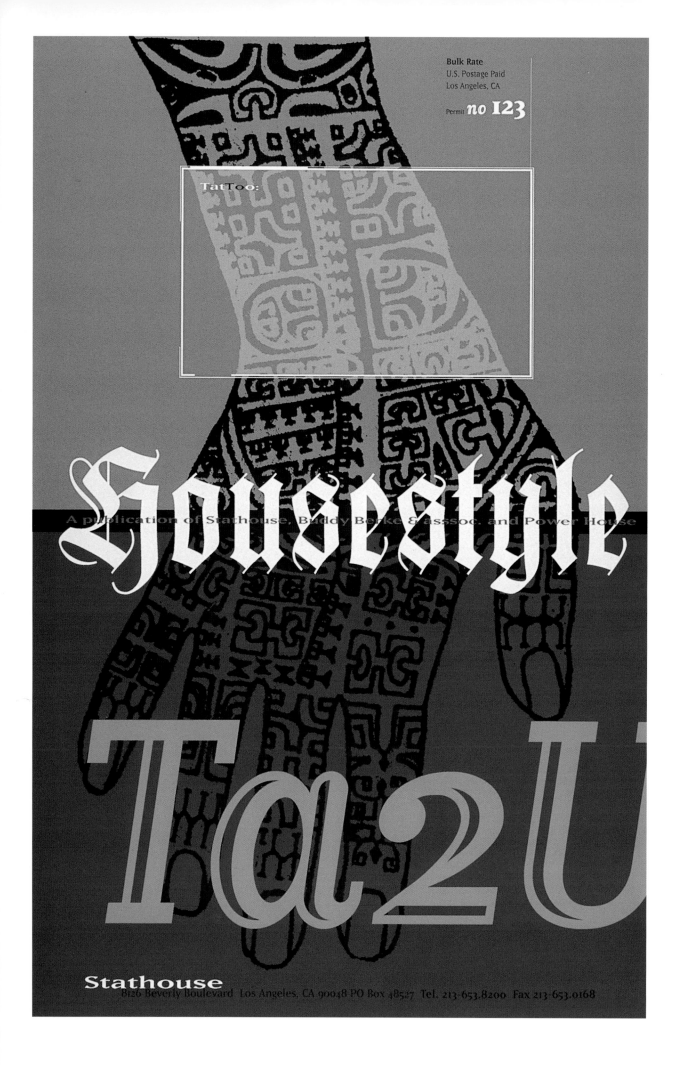

**Bulk Rate**
U.S. Postage Paid
Los Angeles, CA

Permit **no 123**

TatToo:

# Housestyle

A publication of Stathouse, Buddy Berke & asssoc. and Power House

# Ta2U

**Stathouse**
8126 Beverly Boulevard  Los Angeles, CA 90048 PO Box 48527  Tel. 213-653.8200  Fax 213-653.0168

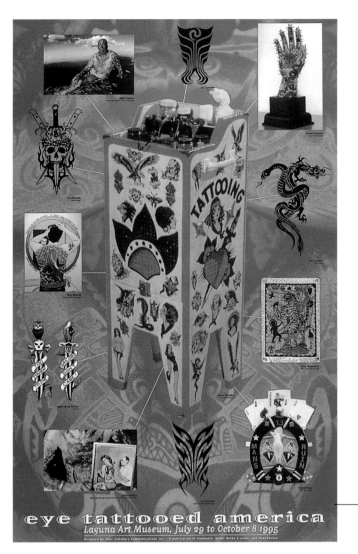

DESIGN   Mike Salisbury, Sander van Baalen, and Sander Egging
         for Mike Salisbury Communications, Inc.
PROJECT  Housestyle newsletter
CLIENT   Stat House/Power House
TOOLS    QuarkXPress, Adobe Illustrator, Adobe Photoshop on Macintosh
FONTS    Matrix, Wilhelm Klingspor Gotisch

This is the design for **the premiere issue** of a quarterly newsletter published by Stat House (a **digital** and conventional service bureau) featuring **Los Angeles design and art events**. The designers chose the type to reflect the **theme of this issue: tattoo art.**

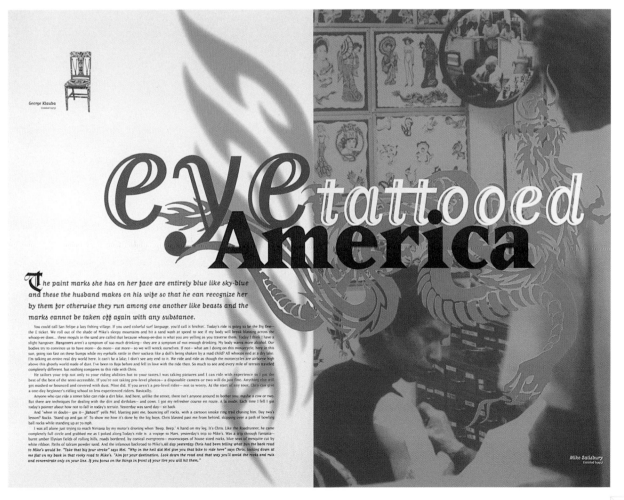

DESIGN    Carlos Segura for Segura, Inc.
PROJECT    1996 XXX Snowboards catalog cover
CLIENT    XXX
TOOLS    Adobe Illustrator, Adobe Photoshop, QuarkXPress
FONT    Proton

This year, the catalog took the shape of a **trip diary, planner**, calendar, **snowboard tips and ethical guidelines**, travel information, and resort, car, and airline 800 numbers.

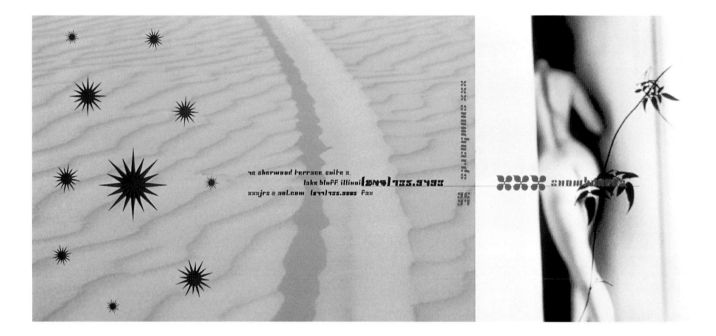

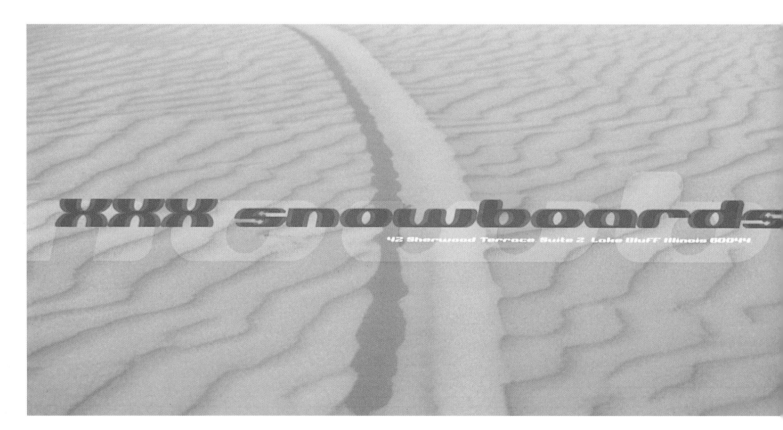

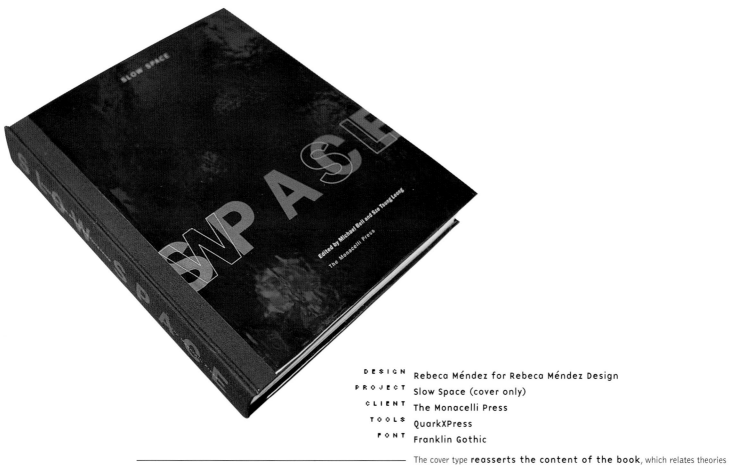

DESIGN   Rebeca Méndez for Rebeca Méndez Design
PROJECT   Slow Space (cover only)
CLIENT   The Monacelli Press
TOOLS   QuarkXPress
FONT   Franklin Gothic

The cover type **reasserts the content of the book**, which relates theories of time, the city, and "authentic architectural experience."

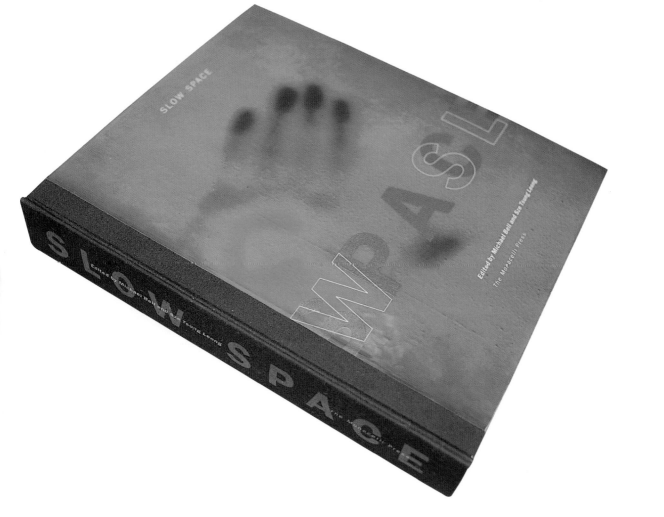

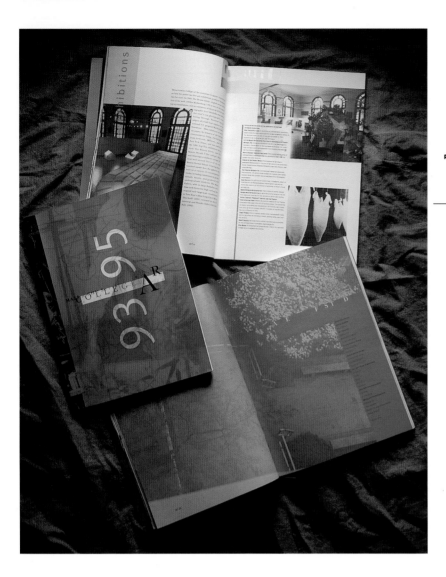

DESIGN Clifford Stoltze, Kyong Choe, Rebecca Fagan,
and Peter Farrell for Stoltze Design
PROJECT Massachusetts College of Art 93-95 catalog
CLIENT Massachusetts College of Art
FONTS Meta, New Baskerville, Trixie

Baskerville and Meta are incorporated to **suggest
the old and the new, which contrast
with Trixie** used for student quotes.

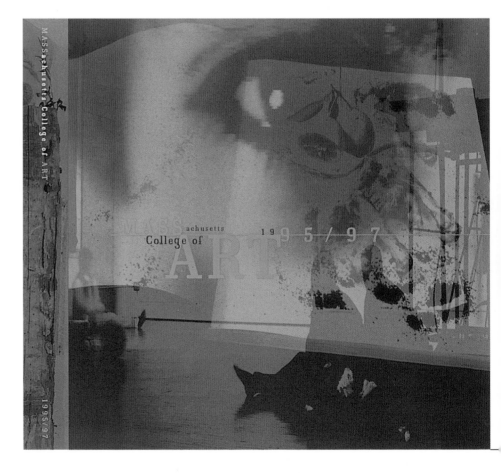

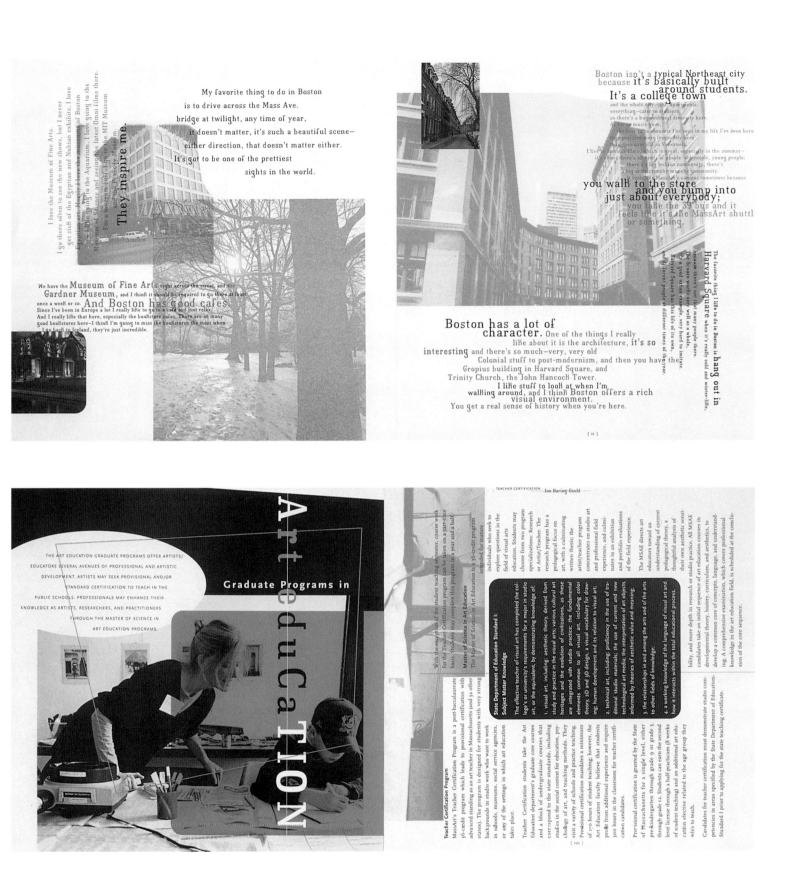

My favorite thing to do in Boston is to drive across the Mass Ave. bridge at twilight, any time of year, it doesn't matter, it's such a beautiful scene— either direction, that doesn't matter either. It's got to be one of the prettiest sights in the world.

They inspire me.

I love the Museum of Fine Arts. I go there often to see the new shows, but I never get sick of the Egyptian and Nubian exhibits. I love Egyptian art. I love the Aquarium. I love going to the Museum of Science and seeing the latest Omni films there. I like going to the Aquarium. I love going to the MIT Museum and the Peabody Museum. I'm a museum buff. I go to the

We have the Museum of Fine Arts right across the street, and the Gardner Museum, and I think it should be required to go there at least once a week or so. And Boston has good cafes. Since I've been in Europe a lot I really like to go to a cafe and just relax. And I really like that here, especially the bookstore cafes. There are so many good bookstores here—I think I'm going to miss the bookstores the most when I go back to Iceland, they're just incredible.

Boston isn't a typical Northeast city because it's basically built around students. It's a college town and the whole city—job apartments, everything—cater to students, so there's a huge cultural diversity here. As far as music goes, the best salsa concerts I've seen in my life I've seen here, three percent more frequently here than they ever did in Venezuela. I live in Jamaica Plain, which is great, especially in the summer— it's great there's a variety of people: old people, young people; there's a big lesbian community, there's a big artist-crunchy-munchy community.

you walk to the store and you bump into just about everybody; you take the 39 bus and it feels like it's the MassArt shuttl or something.

The favorite thing I like to do in Boston is hang out in Harvard Square when it's really cold and winter-like, because there's not that many people there. The Square works very well as a whole. It's a good urban example, very hard to imitate. Harvard Square has this life of its own, and different people at different times of the year.

Boston has a lot of character. One of the things I really like about it is the architecture, it's so interesting and there's so much—very, very old Colonial stuff to post-modernism, and then you have Gropius building in Harvard Square, and Trinity Church, the John Hancock Tower. I like stuff to look at when I'm walking around, and I think Boston offers a rich visual environment. You get a real sense of history when you're here.

[ 11 ]

THE ART EDUCATION GRADUATE PROGRAMS OFFER ARTISTS/
EDUCATORS SEVERAL AVENUES OF PROFESSIONAL AND ARTISTIC
DEVELOPMENT. ARTISTS MAY SEEK PROVISIONAL AND/OR
STANDARD CERTIFICATION TO TEACH IN THE
PUBLIC SCHOOLS. PROFESSIONALS MAY ENHANCE THEIR
KNOWLEDGE AS ARTISTS, RESEARCHERS, AND PRACTITIONERS
THROUGH THE MASTER OF SCIENCE IN
ART EDUCATION PROGRAMS.

Graduate Programs in

Art EducaTION

**Teacher Certification Program**
MassArt's Teacher Certification Program is a post-baccalaureate 36-credit program which leads to provisional certification with advanced standing as an art teacher in Massachusetts (and 32 other states). The program is designed for students with very strong backgrounds in studio work who want to work in schools, museums, social service agencies, or any of the settings in which art education takes place.

Teacher Certification students take the Art Education department's graduate core courses and a block of undergraduate courses that correspond to the state standards, including studies in the social content for education, psychology of art, and teaching methods. They visit a variety of schools and practice teaching. Provisional certification mandates a minimum of 110 hours of student teaching; however, the Art Education faculty believe that students profit from additional experience and require 300 hours in the classroom for teacher certification candidates.

Provisional certification is granted by the State of Massachusetts for a single level, either pre-kindergarten through grade 9 or grade 5 through grade 12. Students can earn the second level license through a half-practicum (8 weeks of student teaching) and an additional art education elective related to the age group they wish to teach.

[ 100 ]

With the exception of the student teaching semester, course work for the Teacher Certification program can be taken on a part-time basis. Students may complete this program in a year and a half.

**Master of Science in Art Education**
The Master of Science in Art Education is a 36-credit program intended for mature individuals who seek to explore questions in the field of visual arts education. Students may choose from two program specializations: Research or Artist/Teacher. The research program has a pedagogical focus on art, with a culminating written thesis; the artist/teacher program concentrates on studio art and professional field experience, and culminates in an exhibition and portfolio evaluations of the field experience.

The MSAE directs art educators toward an understanding of current pedagogical theory, a thoughtful analysis of their own aesthetic sensibility, and more depth in research or studio practice. All MSAE candidates take an initial sequence of art education courses in developmental theory, history, curriculum, and aesthetics, to develop a common core of concepts, language, and understanding. A comprehensive examination, which covers professional knowledge in the art education field, is scheduled at the conclusion of the core sequence.

Candidates for teacher certification must demonstrate studio competencies in areas specified by the State Department of Education. Standard I prior to applying for the state teaching certificate.

TEACHER CERTIFICATION   Jon Baring-Gould

**State Department of Education Standard I:**
**Subject Matter Knowledge**

The effective teacher of visual art has completed the college's or university's requirements for a major in studio art, or the equivalent, by demonstrating knowledge of:

1. visual art, including: aesthetic theory, derived from study and practice in the visual arts; various cultural art heritages and the evolution of civilization, as these are integrated with studio practice; the fundamental elements common to all visual art, including color theory, 2D and 3D design, a visual vocabulary for drawing; human development and its relation to visual art;

2. technical art, including: proficiency in the use of traditional studio materials; the use of current and new technological art media; the interpretation of art objects informed by theories of aesthetic value and meaning;

3. the relationships in and among the arts and of the arts to other fields of knowledge;

4. a working knowledge of the language of visual art and how it interacts within the total educational process.

DESIGN  Clifford Stoltze, Tracey Schroeder, Heather Kramer, Peter Farrell, and Resa Blatman for Stoltze Design
PROJECT  Massachusetts College of Art 95-97 catalog
CLIENT  Massachusetts College of Art
FONTS  Scala Sans Serif, Scala Serif, Calvino

Scala Sans Serif and Scala Serif are used with Calvino, adding a **more expressive personal voice** to the student quotes.

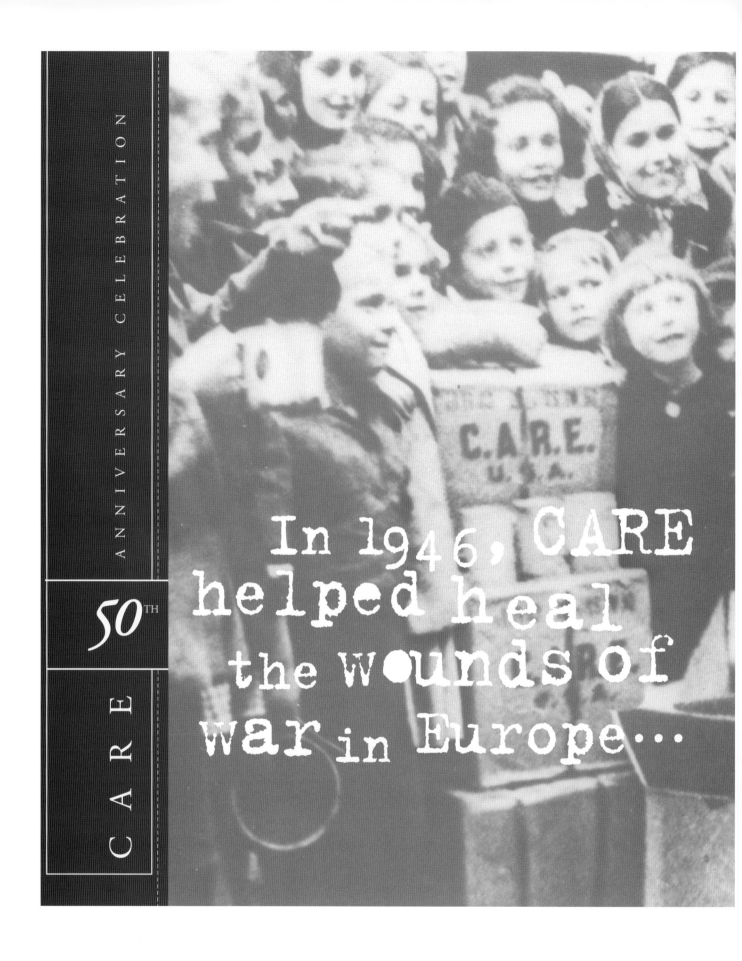

In 1946, CARE helped heal the wounds of war in Europe...

<br>

**A PROMISE FULFILLED 1946**

# "14 months in a Nazi

## concentration camp was enough to believe that there would not be anyone in the

**world**
**When** they put 100-130 in gas chamber they played outside a waltz or polka — you know the people are dying the worst sort of death. ■ When the night and day shooting, bombing was over, when we found out that our doors were not locked any longer, that — it sounded wonderful but still foreign — that 'we could go home' ■ It was like looking through a heavy fog that I realized that other women climbed in individual private cars, hugged, kissed the driver, cried. Someone, a friend, a relative had arrived, someone was alive. No one looked at me or called my name. ■ I still cannot know or remember who picked me up, where they took me. Neither do I know today how long I was in white, soft bed, who brought me some food, what the

like. ■ After weeks in the hospital the first miracle happened, still I cannot explain it fully. A CARE Package arrived for me. I asked every doctor, nurse, cleaning staff, 'What is CARE? Who brought the package?' Shrugging shoulders and polite silence was the answer. When I opened the package I found a wonderful heavy warm wool blanket. A week or 10 days later came another package, another lighter blanket, milk powder, everything that one needs to make good pancakes. I felt like experiencing a fairy tale, was sort of helpless too because I could never find out the person or organization, so I could say 'Thank you!'"— Interview with Margot Mertens, July 1994

Margot Mertens, the daughter of a successful Jewish architect in Berlin, worked as a radio operator in the resistance movement before being arrested by the SS. After the war, she took a job with RIAS, Radio in the American Sector in occupied Germany and later with Voice of America in New York. Today she lives in Vermont, where she often shares her story with school children.

**A PROMISE RENEWED 1996**

# "I am a Rwandan.

## I was born in Rwimishinya, Kibungo Prefecture, in 1956. I married Kabagwira Caphrose in 1978. We had six children; two daughters and four sons...

**On** April 19, 1994, the civil war in my country forced us to leave our home in Rwimishinya and seek refuge in Tanzania. We walked for over 10 days. It was the rainy season, and because we had no shelter my two daughters contracted pneumonia and died. We remained in the bush for a long time, hoping the war would end. ■ We had run out of food a few days before, and were sure that we would die of starvation. Most of the other refugees were in the same condition — no food, little water, no shelter, sitting in the rain. At this time, our two youngest sons died. Now only our two oldest sons were left, and they were so thin and sick that my wife and I thought that they would not

with us much longer. ■ Finally, help arrived. ■ Very soon, CARE began to set up the Benaco refugee camp, to provide food, 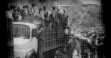 blankets, cooking pots, to build latrines and, with the help of other organizations, provide water and medical care. ■ Myself and my family have lost much in the last year. But we are thankful to be alive. And when our two sons awake in the morning, they are eager to fetch water and firewood to help their mother to prepare the food that CARE provides us. Once more we feel happiness and hope. For these things we must thank CARE." — Interview with Munyantwali

Munyantwali Valens, a Rwandan refugee, told his story to Katabogama Manasse, a CARE worker at the Benaco refugee camp in Tanzania in 1995. Today he and his family are among the hundreds of thousands of Rwandans working — with help from CARE — to rebuild their country and end the cycle of ethnic and tribal violence.

**DESIGN** Richard Berry for CARE Communications
**PROJECT** CARE's 50th Anniversary Journal
**TOOLS** Adobe Photoshop, QuarkXPress on Macintosh
**FONT** Trixie

The original photo prints were scanned in-house, **manipulated in Photoshop**, brought into QuarkXPress, and output directly to film. On the "Concentration Camp" spread and the "Rwanda" spread, the type was **set in a small point size** and **enlarged several generations** on a photocopier. The final copies were scanned into Photoshop, where some additional tweaking was done.

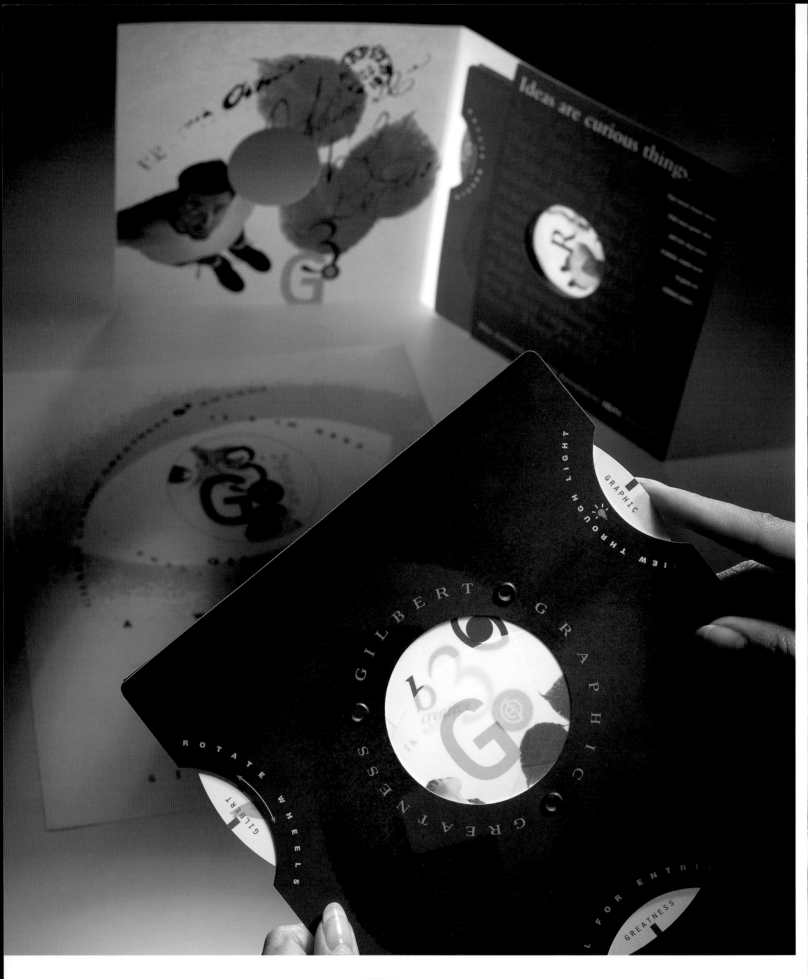

| | |
|---|---|
| DESIGN | Michelle Aranda and Ron Miriello for Miriello Grafico, Inc. |
| PROJECT | Gilbert G3 Awards |
| CLIENT | Gilbert Paper Company |
| TOOLS | Adobe Illustrator, Adobe Photoshop on Macintosh |
| FONTS | Bembo, Helvetica, ITC Kabel |

————— **To reinvigorate the awards program,** a call-for-entries brochure using a turning-wheel design of type and photo images allows for **endless combinations.**

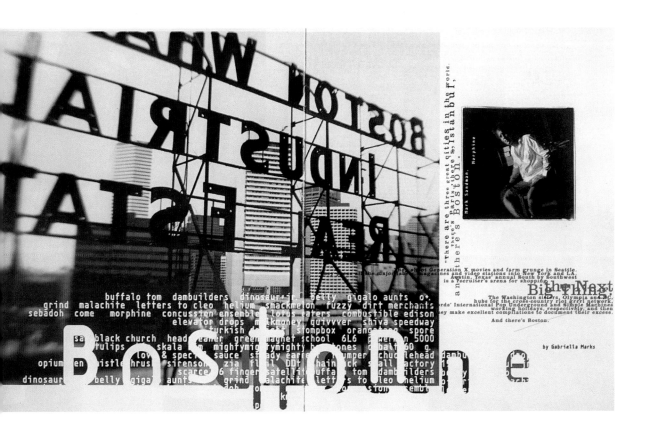

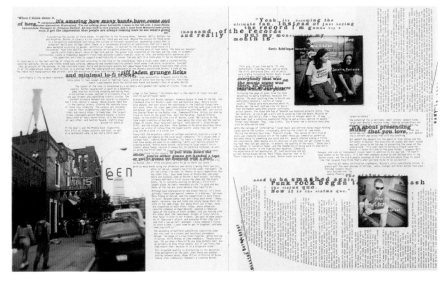

DESIGN    Clifford Stoltze and Peter Farrell for Stoltze Design
PROJECT    Boston Music Scene Feature in *Raygun*, issue 20
CLIENT    *Raygun* Magazine
FONTS    Isonorm, Clarendon

The challenge was to use fonts that **had never been used** in *Raygun* before. **The designers** chose Isonorm and Clarendon to **contrast old and new.**

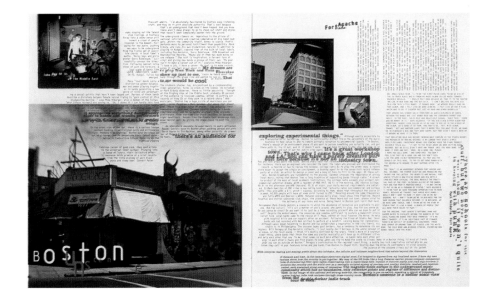

# miscellaneous

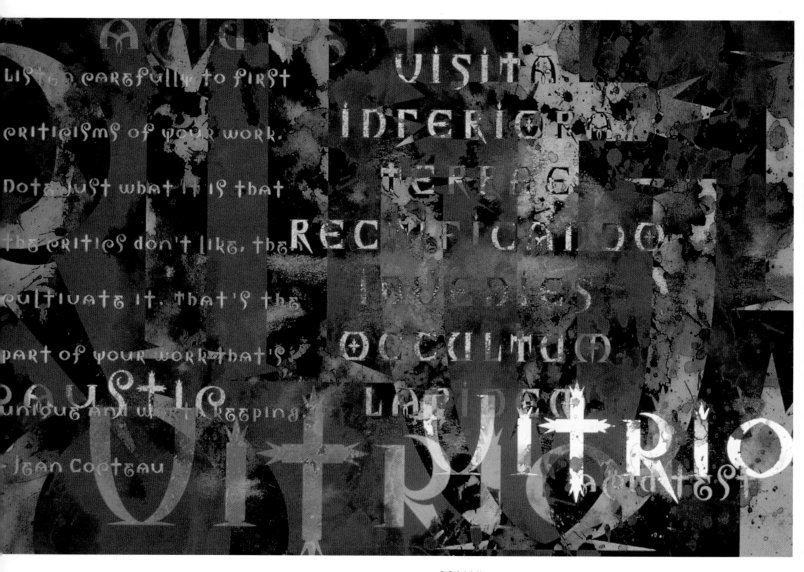

VISITA

INFERIOR

RECTIFICAN DO

OCCULTUM

VITRIOL

Listen carefully to first
criticisms of your work.
Note just what it is that
the critics don't like, then
cultivate it. That's the
part of your work that's
unique and worth keeping.

—Jean Cocteau

**DESIGN** Margo Chase for Margo Chase Design
**TOOLS** Fontographer
**FONT** Vitriol

The **inspiration** for this font was
**Medieval manuscripts** and Gothic versal caps.
The lowercase works as a complete **font** without uppercase.
The designer intended the **capitals** for
ornamental letters only.

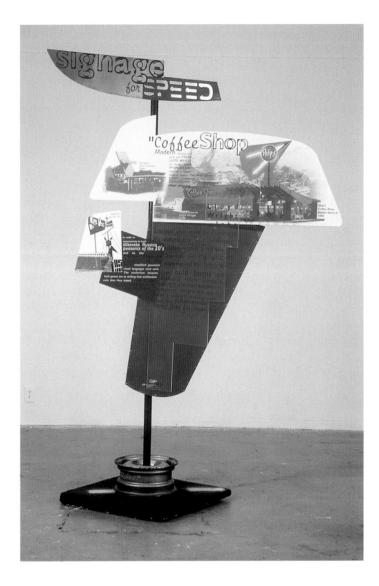

**DESIGN** Todd Childers for Todd Childers Graphic Design
**PROJECT** California Arts MFA Thesis
**TOOLS** Illustrator and Photoshop on Macintosh

This is a portion of a **thesis** concerning the evolution of the **roadside environment** in America.

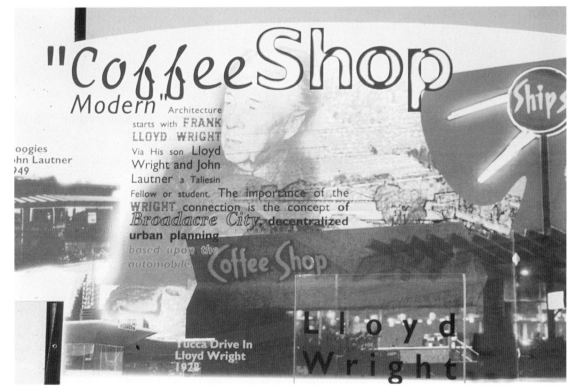

DESIGN   Sander van Baalen and Andre Hanegraaf
CLIENT   Utrecht School of the Arts (H.K.U.)
TOOLS    Font Studio
FONT     Logic

These typeface forms are **based on an I.C. chip** taken from a typesetter made in 1971. The font is **an ode to the new typographic tools.** Each design package includes a disk, a real I.C. chip, and three type example cards: plain, oblique, and oblique extended.

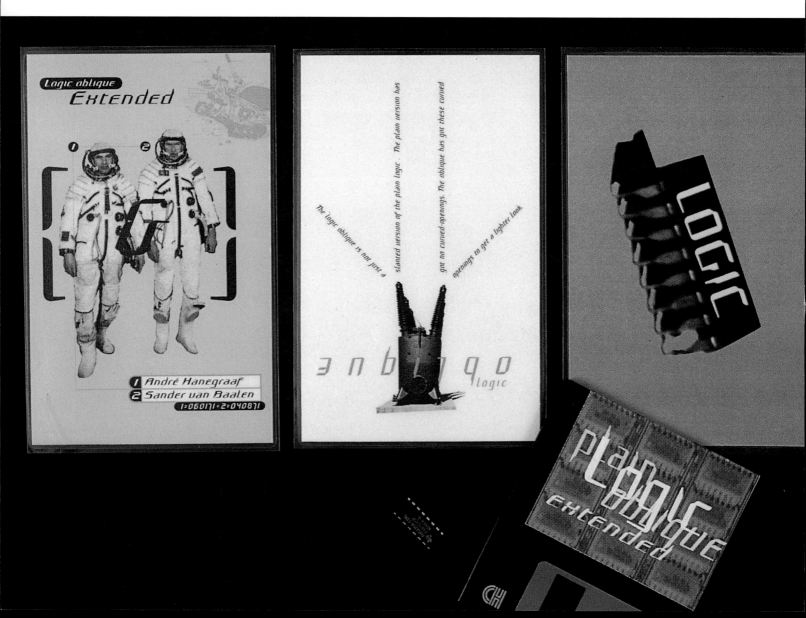

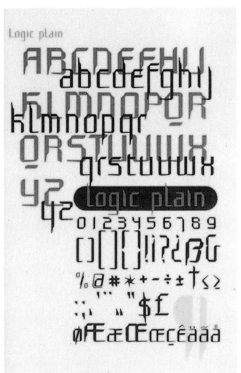

Logic plain

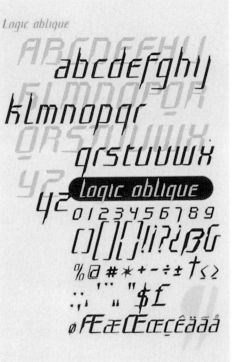

Logic oblique

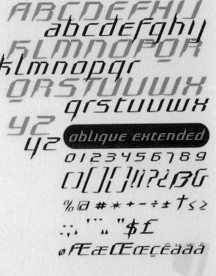

Logic oblique extended

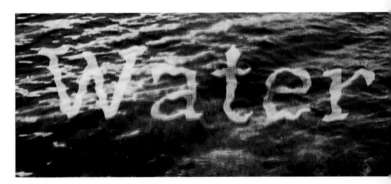

DESIGN    Jure Stojan for Stojan
PROJECT    Type Specimen
TOOLS    Adobe Photoshop on PC
FONT    Pekel Regular

To illustrate creative usage of a new typeface, the designers used **Photoshop's layering feature.** After altering the shapes of the letters, the designers used opacitysliders to **apply transparence** then diffused the image.

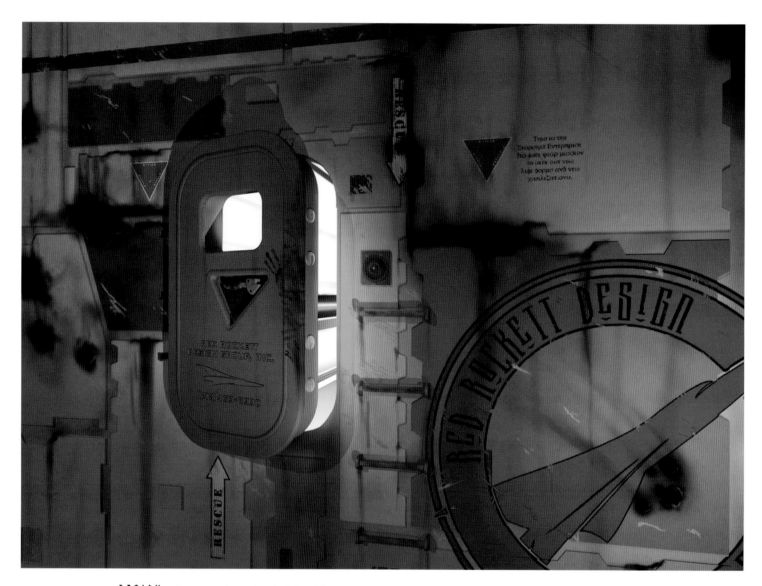

DESIGN    Adam Murguia and Ned Rickett for Red Rockett Design
PROJECT    Promotional pieces
TOOLS    Adobe Illustrator, Adobe Photoshop, Strato Studio Pro
FONTS    Eurostile Extended, Stencil, Kells, Halfway House, Symbol

The design was created with Illustrator and Photoshop, and Strata Studio Pro was used to **add dimension.**

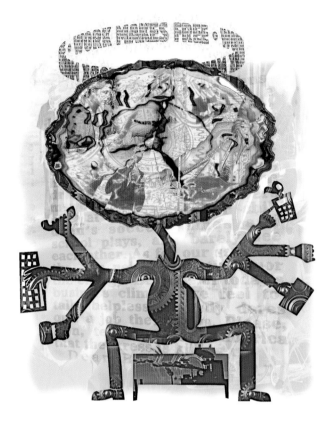

DESIGN  Kelly Brother for Kelly Brother Illustration
PROJECT  Work Makes Free
TOOLS  Adobe Illustrator, Adobe Photoshop on Macintosh
FONTS  Newspaper Clippings, Block Condensed

This piece is a **visual commentary on corporate downsizing** and overworked laborers. Some of the **images** were taken from a CD-ROM, while others were **scanned.** The illustration was then opened in Photoshop, where **textures, colors, and layers** were added. The head was created by **scanning the face of a clock.**

DESIGN  Kelly Brother for Kelly Brother Illustration
PROJECT  Wrestlers
TOOLS  Adobe Illustrator, Adobe Photoshop on Macintosh
FONTS  Newspaper Clippings, Block Condensed

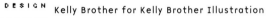

This piece is a visual commentary on **hostile land wars.** A hand-drawn map and headlines from various newspapers were scanned to **create the textures and layers of meaning.** The airbrush tool, set to **"dissolve,"** was used extensively to create texture. The "alien" creature signifies the **alien aspects of mankind.**

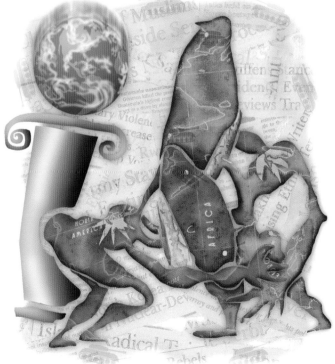

DESIGN   Rich Godfrey for FUSE, Inc.
PROJECT  DiVitale advertisement
CLIENT   DiVitale Photography
TOOLS    Adobe Illustrator, Adobe Photoshop, Fontographer
FONT     Letter Gothic

This font was designed to **create a visual identity** for a photographer.

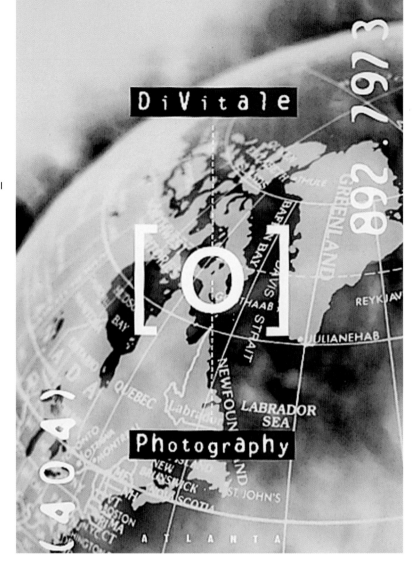

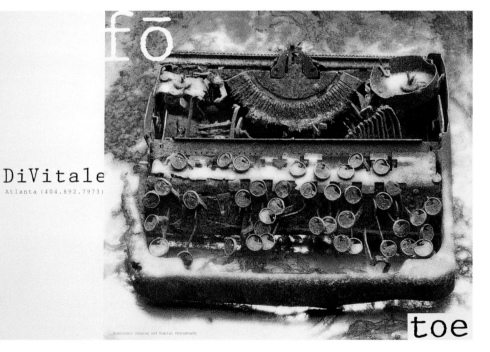

DESIGN   Rich Godfrey for FUSE, Inc.
PROJECT  DiVitale advertisement
CLIENT   DiVitale Photography
TOOLS    Adobe Illustrator, Adobe Photoshop, Fontographer on Macintosh
FONT     Scan from a manual typewriter

The typewriter font was chosen **to be consistent** with the image of an old typewriter.

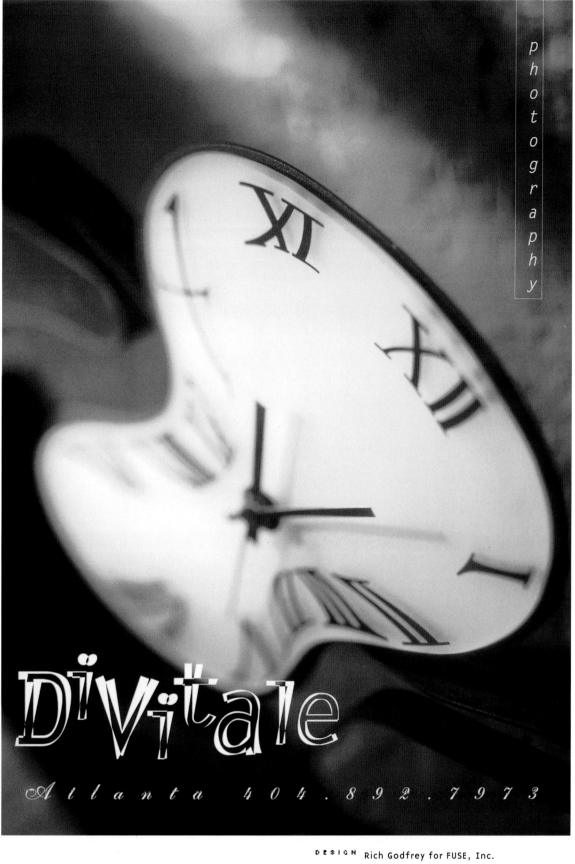

Divitale

*Atlanta 404.892.7973*

| | |
|---|---|
| **DESIGN** | Rich Godfrey for FUSE, Inc. |
| **PROJECT** | Photo Source Book advertisement |
| **CLIENT** | Divitale Photography |
| **TOOLS** | Illustrator and Photoshop on Macintosh |

This font was **created** by masking
a roman **letter** into an italic letter of the same **font**.

You see someone you know in a large crowd...

after talking to them

yo u

su ddenly realize how

small this place is in which we live.

DESIGN Rich Godfrey for FUSE, Inc.
PROJECT DiVitale advertisement—black book promotion
CLIENT DiVitale Photography
TOOLS Adobe Illustrator, Adobe Photoshop, Fontographer
FONT Letter Gothic

This is an ad done for a black book promotion in which DiVitale was the photographer. The designer **wanted the type and the image to look similar** so that people would **connect** the ad and the promo.

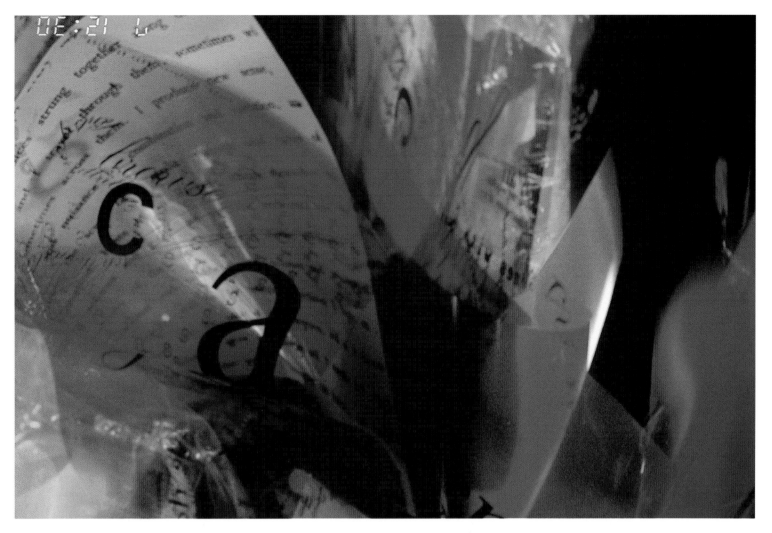

DESIGN Deborah Littlejohn
PROJECT Imagery for self-authored essay on digital media
TOOLS Photoshop
FONTS OCRA, Künstler Script, Baskerville

These images were generated to accompany
an essay on digital typography meant to be **read, viewed, and experienced on a computer screen.**
The fluid, animated, **three-dimensional world** of the computer needs dynamic,
three-dimensional typography. Filters, lights, gels, and **35mm film captured the text** printed on cellophane,
vellum, and Mylar. The photos were further manipulated in Photoshop.

DESIGN   Margo Chase for Margo Chase Design
TOOLS   Fontographer
FONT   Envision

Envision was designed as a **contemporary** version of uncial alphabets. The designer based the forms on uncial and "**symbol**" fonts and the **proportions on Palatino.**

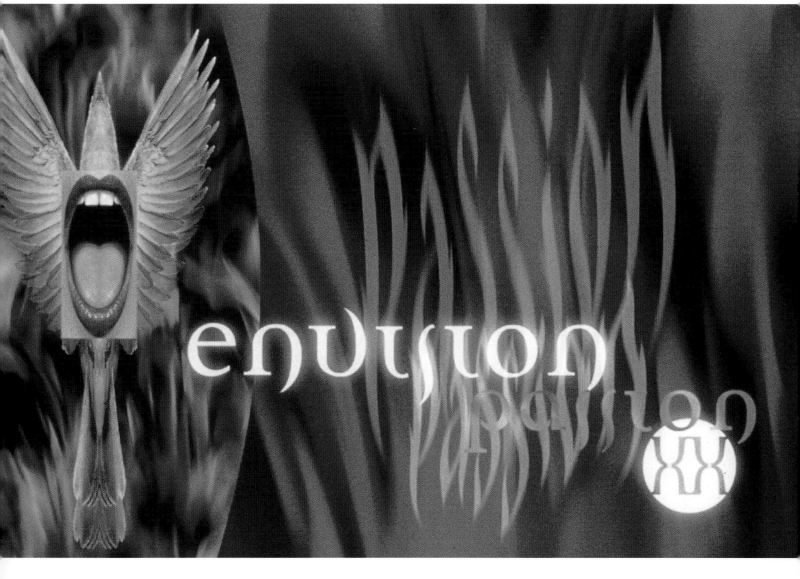

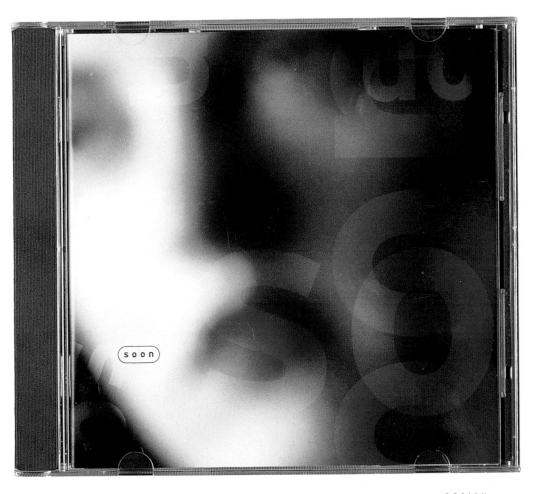

DESIGN    Fritz Klaetke for Visual Dialogue
PROJECT   Soon CD packaging
CLIENT    CVB Studios
TOOLS     Adobe Photoshop, QuarkXPress on Macintosh
FONT      Interstate

Type subtly overlays an **out-of-focus photo** that conveys
the **general mood** of this collection of songs.
The CD is used as a **promotion for bands and illustrators**
and is sold with all proceeds going to the Aids Action Committee in Boston.

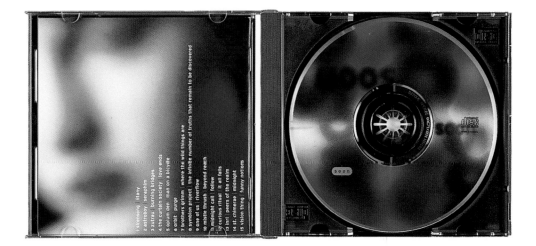

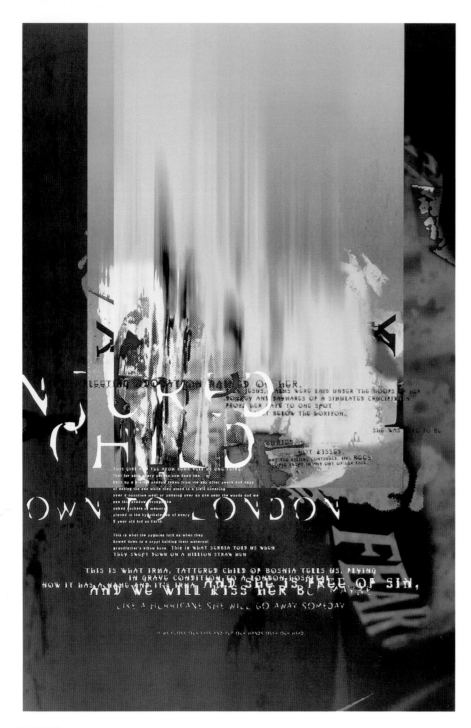

**DESIGN** Stephen Farrell for SLIP
**PROJECT** Injured Child Flown to London
**TOOLS** Adobe Photoshop, QuarkXPress, Adobe Illustrator, Fontographer on Macintosh
**FONTS** Commonworld, Entropy, Stamp Gothic

An example of text illustrating the typeface in which it appears. Both **comment on brokenness:**
the poem on the **broken social and political structures** of Europe, and the typeface
on the **fractured nature** of communication in English.
Commonworld was developed from Garamond and Industry Sans, and Entropy is from Missive and Carmella.

**DESIGN** Stephen Farrell for SLIP
**PROJECT** Place is Assemblage is Display Type
**CLIENT** *Confetti* magazine
**TOOLS** Adobe Photoshop, QuarkXPress, Adobe Illustrator, Fontographer on Macintosh
**FONTS** Missive, Entropy, Osprey

The three typefaces are **derivations of one another,** inspired by the designer's move
to an urban environment. The montage forms, modeled from bits
of **type design spanning 400 years,** serve as snapshots of complexity and contradiction,
a framing device for the **designer's current surroundings.**

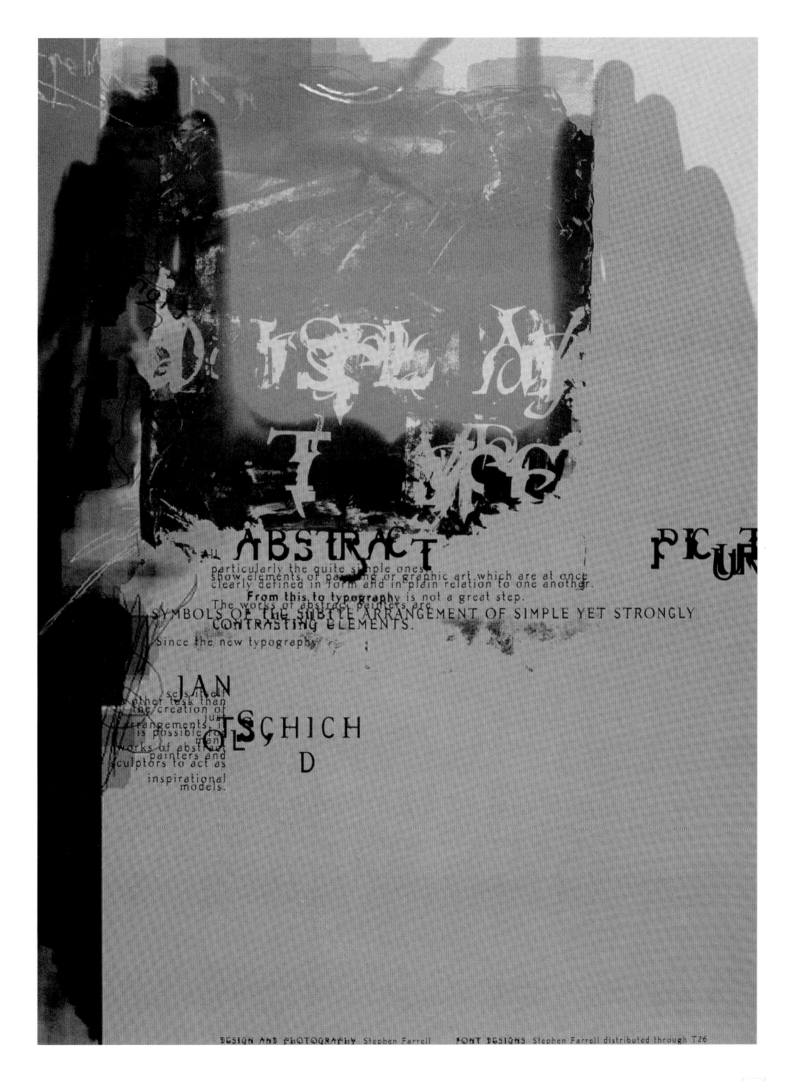

DISPLAY TYPE

ABSTRACT                                          PICTUR

ALL particularly the quite simple ones
show elements of painting or graphic art which are at once
clearly defined in form and in plain relation to one another.
**From this to typography** is not a great step.
The works of abstract painters are
SYMBOLS OF THE SUBTLE ARRANGEMENT OF SIMPLE YET STRONGLY
CONTRASTING ELEMENTS.

Since the new typography

sets itself
no other task than
the creation of
arrangements, it
is possible man
works of abstract
painters and
sculptors to act as
inspirational
models.

JAN
TSCHICH
OLD

DESIGN AND PHOTOGRAPHY Stephen Farrell          FONT DESIGNS Stephen Farrell distributed through T26

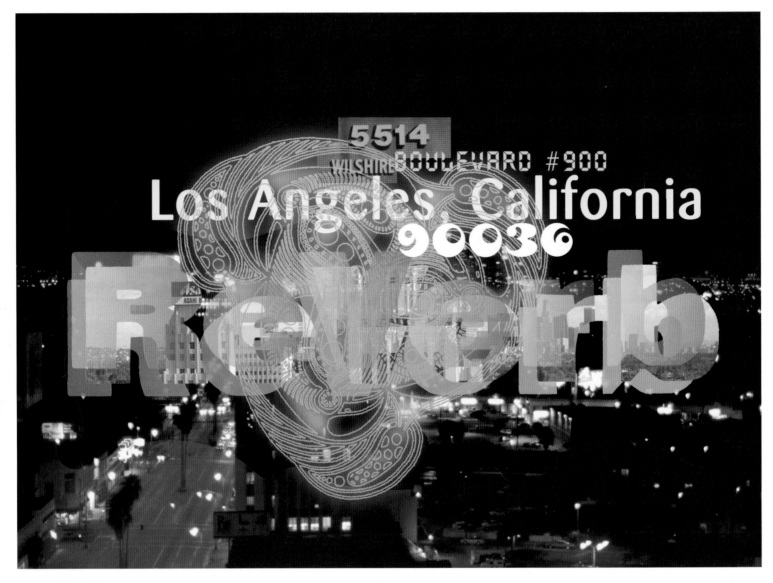

5514
WILSHIRE BOULEVARD #900
Los Angeles, California
90036
ReVerb

DESIGN Somi Kim for ReVerb
PROJECT ReVerb postcard
TOOLS Adobe Photoshop, QuarkXPress on Macintosh
FONT Unidentified American wood type, late nineteenth century

Type from **a variety of sources** was juxtaposed
to create a **multilevel view facing downtown** Los Angeles from the east windows of the studio.
The font (known as Font Doe) was **originally hand set** and printed on a letterpress
in an unidentified antique wood font purchased by Harvard's Bow and Arrow Press from Thomas Todd
Printers, Boston.

DESIGN    Masaki Fujimoto for Peter Piper Graphics
CLIENT    Blue
TOOLS     Adobe Photoshop on Macintosh
FONT      Peignot

This is the **lyric card** for the cd.

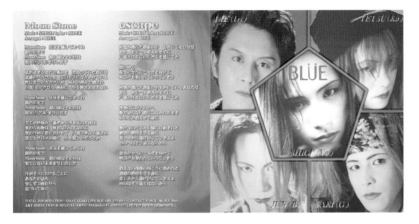

DESIGN    Masaki Fujimoto for Peter Piper Graphics
PROJECT   Demo tape package design
CLIENT    Blue
TOOLS     Adobe Illustrator, Adobe Photoshop
FONT      Emigre Template

This work is designed for a **music tape case**.

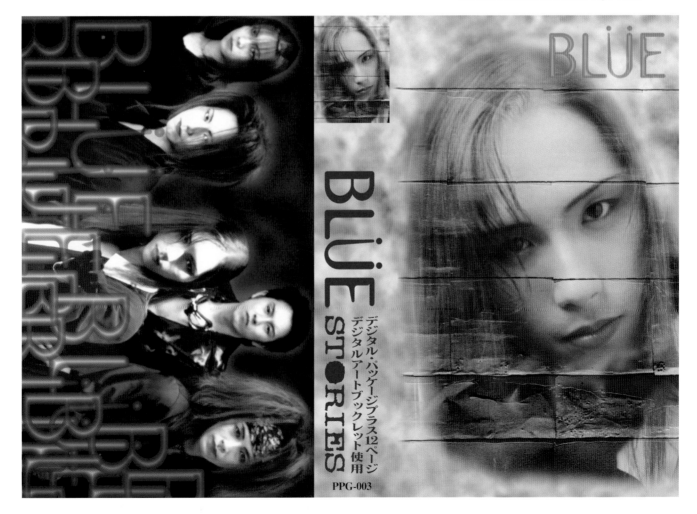

DESIGN    Carolyn Steinbeck for Frau Steinbeck Design
PROJECT    *Die Welt ist schön. Der Ball ist rund*
CLIENT    L.A. Galerie, Frankfurt, Germany
TOOLS    Adobe Photoshop, QuarkXPress on Macintosh
FONT    Prestige Elite

This project is an invitation to a **photography show.** The **designer's loose translation** of the project title is: "The world is beautiful. The ball is round." The second sentence is a quote from a famous German soccer coach that refers to the fact that a **soccer ball** has its undeniable **rules because of its roundness.**

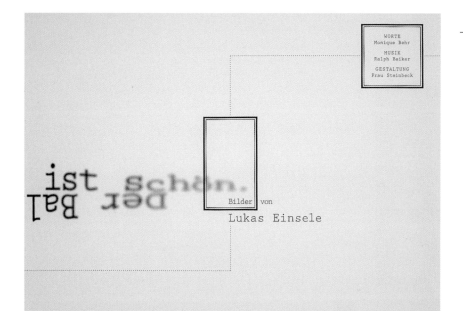

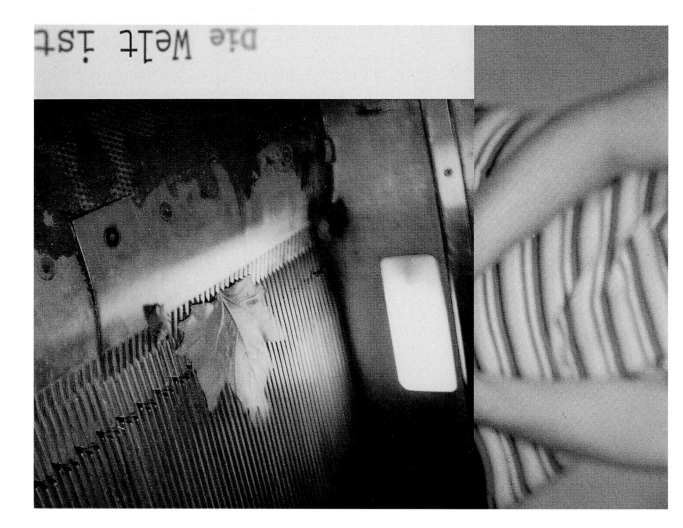

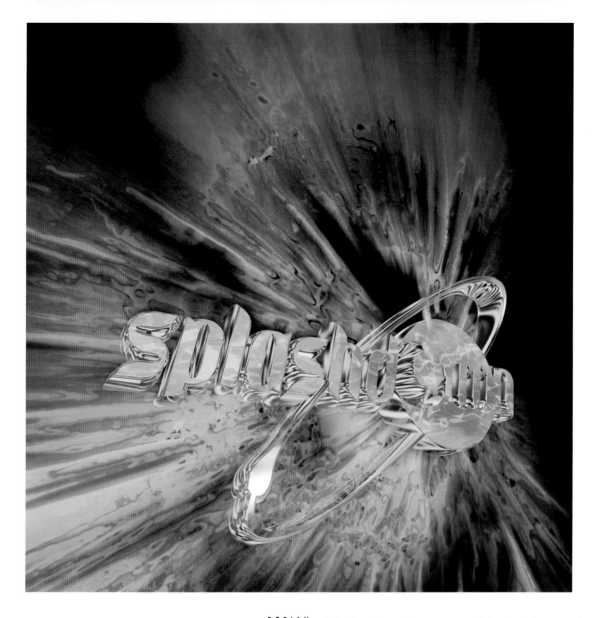

DESIGN   Clifford Stoltze, Wing Ip Ngan, Richard Leighton, and Joe Polevy for Stoltze Design
PROJECT  Splashdown CD *Stars and Guitars*
CLIENT   Castle von Buhler (CVB) Records
TOOLS    QuarkXPress, Adobe Illustrator, Adobe Photoshop, Pixar Typestry on PC
FONTS    Baseline, Cyberotica, Isonorm

The Splashdown logo was initially developed with a **custom font** as flat illustrator art
and then made into a **3-D version** (used the front cover of the cd) in Pixar Typestry.

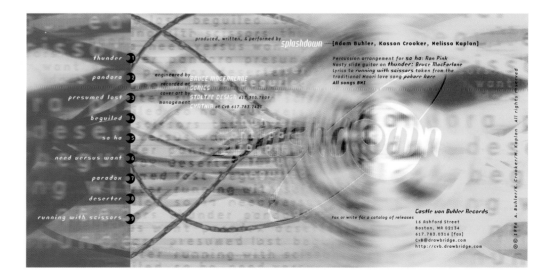

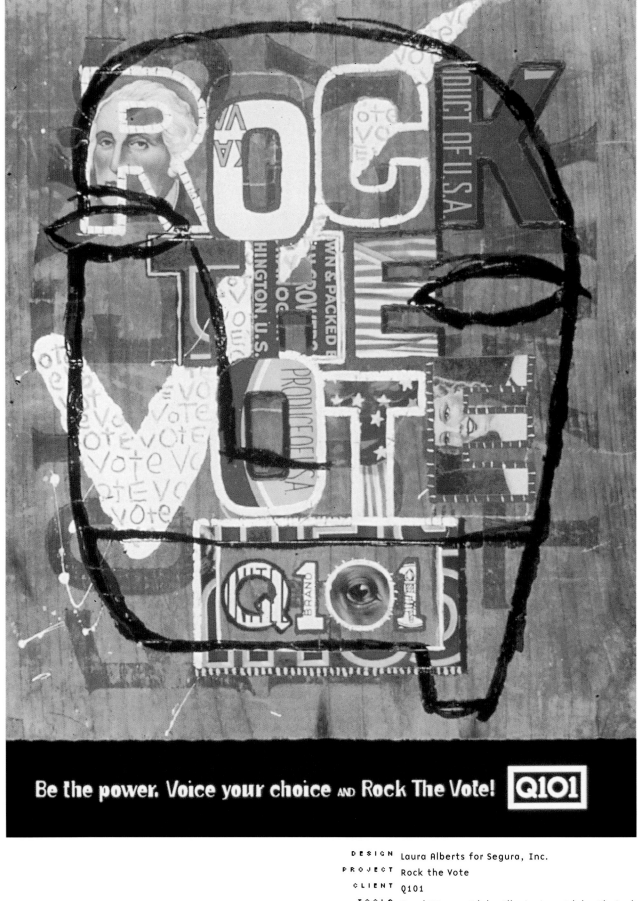

Be the power. Voice your choice AND Rock The Vote! Q101

DESIGN Laura Alberts for Segura, Inc.

PROJECT Rock the Vote

CLIENT Q101

TOOLS QuarkXPress, Adobe Illustrator, Adobe Photoshop

FONT Colonist

Q101 Radio in Chicago is a sponsor for **Rock the Vote.**

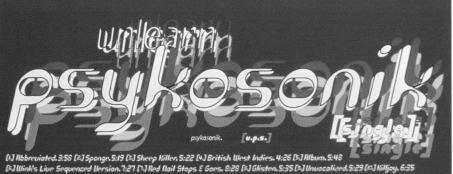

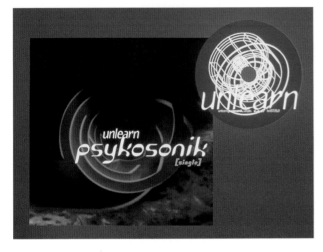

DESIGN  Carlos Segura for Segura, Inc.
PROJECT  Psykosonik
CLIENT  TVT Records
TOOLS  QuarkXPress, Adobe Illustrator, Adobe Photoshop
FONT  Cyberotics, Truth

This is the **CD campaign** for Psykosonik.

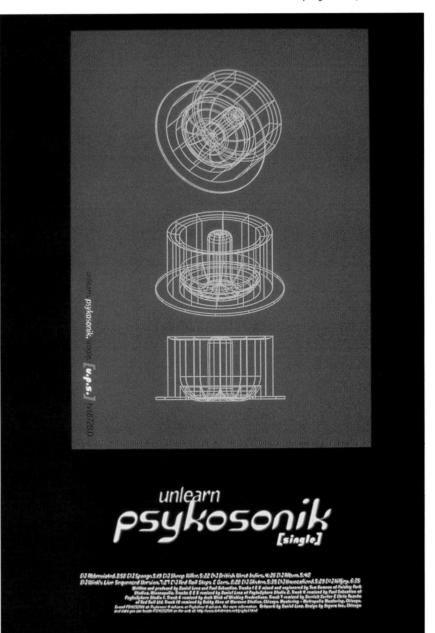

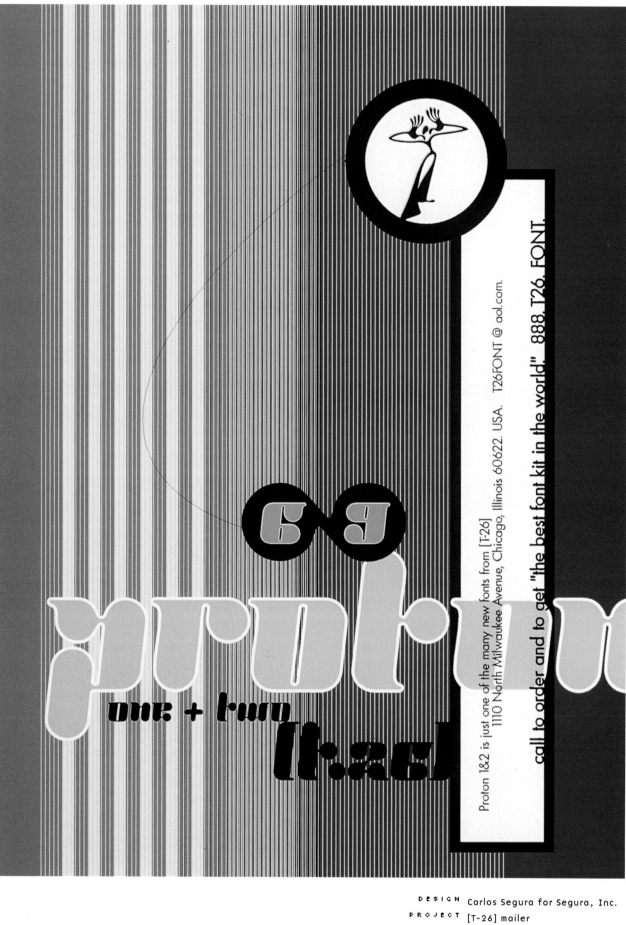

69

proton
one + two
ft:26]

Proton 1&2 is just one of the many new fonts from [T-26]
1110 North Milwaukee Avenue, Chicago, Illinois 60622. USA. T26FONT @ aol.com.
call to order and to get "the best font kit in the world." 888.T26. FONT.

DESIGN Carlos Segura for Segura, Inc.
PROJECT [T-26] mailer
CLIENT [T-26]
TOOLS QuarkXPress, Adobe Illustrator
FONT Proton

This is a postcard **promoting** one of the type foundry's new releases called proton.

DESIGN   Rick Salzman for re: salzman designs
PROJECT  Ski/Abstr 4 advertisement
TOOLS    FreeHand on Macintosh

The abstract shapes and copy **suggest the freedom of downhill skiing** and the need to take a chance by **stepping out of the lines.** The piece was created using client-provided photos, which were modified in Photoshop and composited in FreeHand.

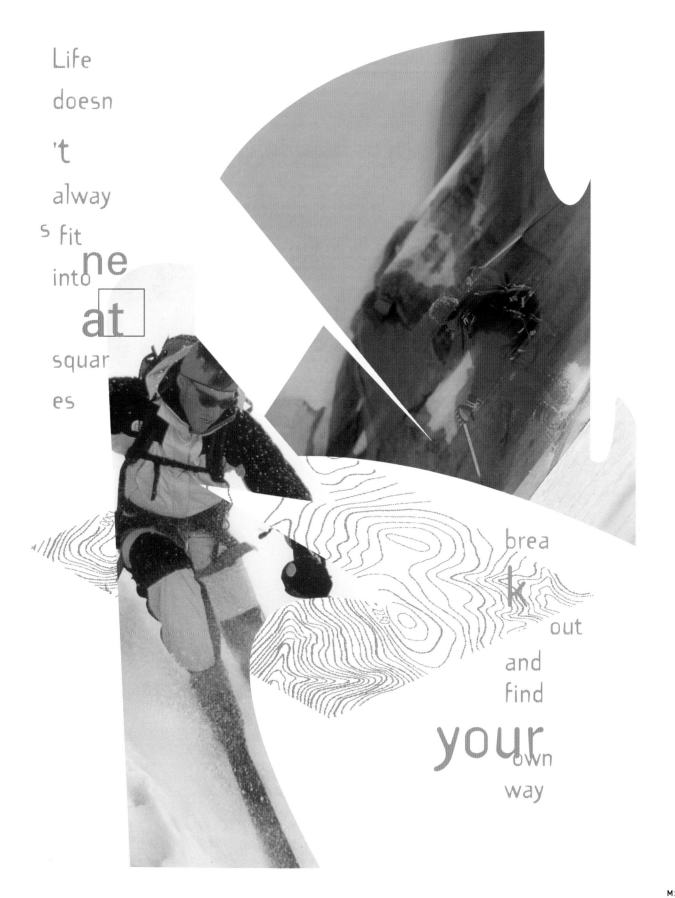

Life doesn 't alway s fit into ne at squar es

brea k out and find your own way

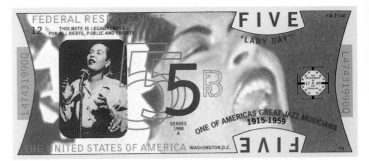

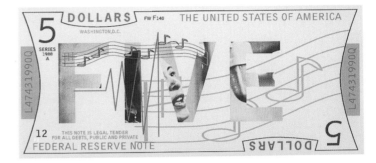

**DESIGN**  Blaine Todd Childers for Todd Childers Graphic Design
**PROJECT**  Learning from Canyon Country
**TOOLS**  Adobe Illustrator, Adobe Photoshop

This is a student project created during
the designer's **graduate studies at CalArts.**

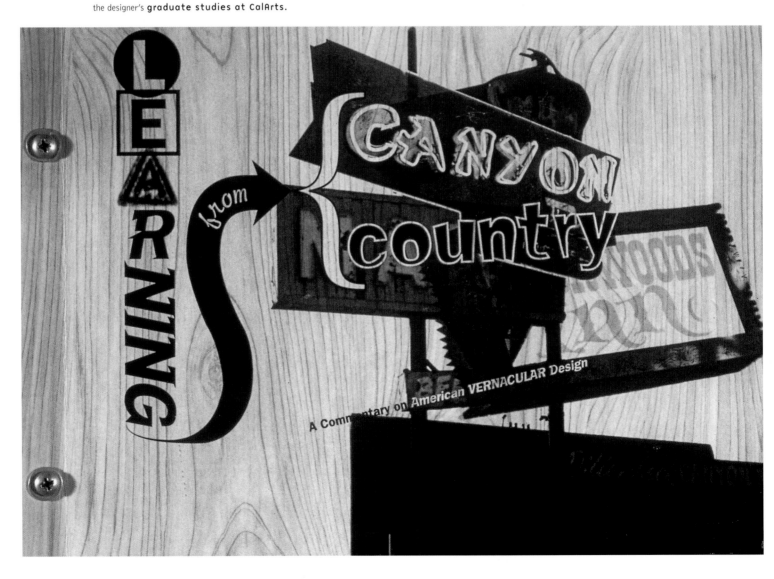

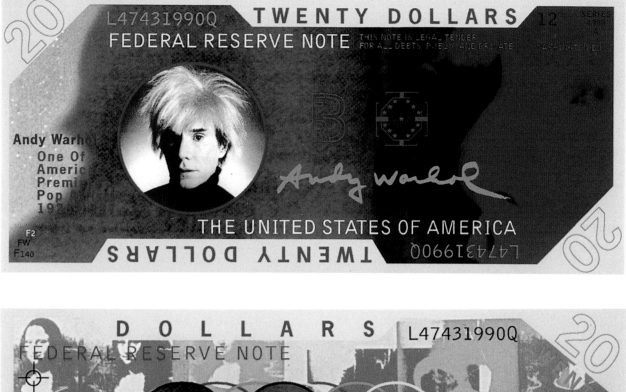

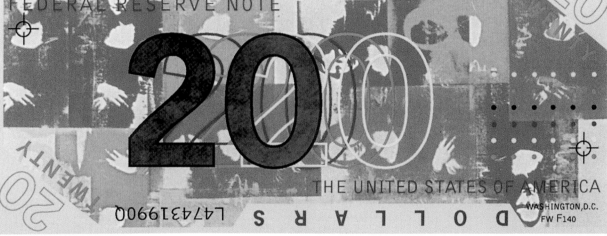

DESIGN    James Stoecker
PROJECT   Cal Arts M.F.A. thesis. $20 and $5 Bills
TOOLS     FreeHand, Adobe Photoshop
FONTS     News Gothic, Bell Gothic

Our currency is very old and lacks expressionism, fun, charm, and warmth.
Color differentiation and form bring numerical heroes in the arts
the acknowledgment they deserve and add to the fabric of American culture.

DESIGN    Carolyn Steinbeck for Cranbrook Academy of Art
PROJECT   *Amerika mon amour or The Forbidden Fruit*
TOOLS     Adobe Illustrator, Adobe Photoshop, QuarkXPress on Macintosh
FONTS     Script Bold, Wittenberger Fractur, Joanna Italic, Chicago

This is a thesis **project for the Cranbrook Academy of Art.**
The design of this thesis **revolves around two** statements,
one is the **Catechism of Influences**, the other is a portion of the designer's thesis.

AMERIKA
mon amour

# The Forbidden Fruit

(Frau Steinbeck's Platitudes, inspired by Luther's 95 Theses)
An everyday dictionary of steadily asked and
never really answered questions

a f s t e i e n p g

answering
Questions about
Definition
Value
Perfection
Greatness
Soul
Destiny
Force
Companion
Context
Sensation
Performance
Present
Seduction
Pleasure

# V.
## Catechism of Women and Men

incl. Platitudes 57-70

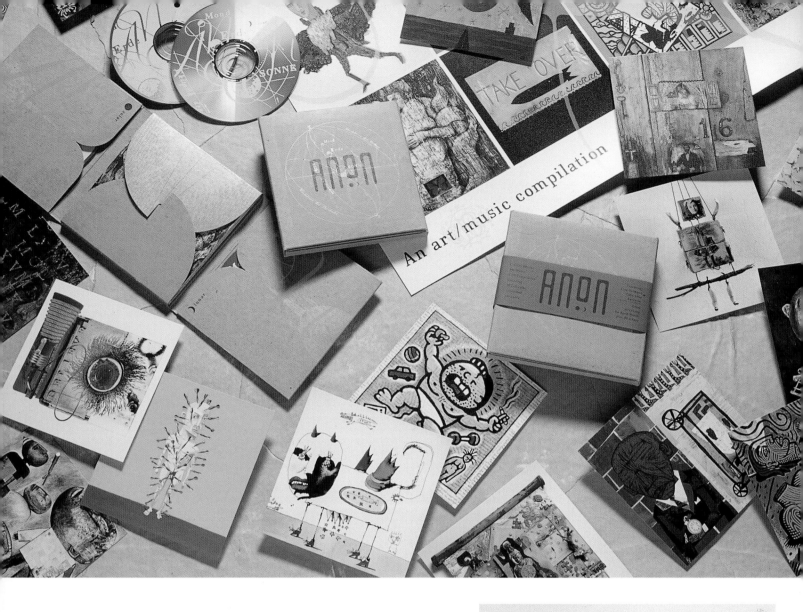

**DESIGN**   Clifford Stoltze for Stoltze Design
**PROJECT**   Anon compilation CD and poster
**CLIENT**   CVB Records

The Anon logo is a **slightly modified** version of an unreleased typeface called Gangly, designed by Joe Polevy. The script font was first set on the computer using the font Amazone and then **photocopied to give it a hand-drawn effect.** Calvino, designed by Elliot Earl, was used for the text.

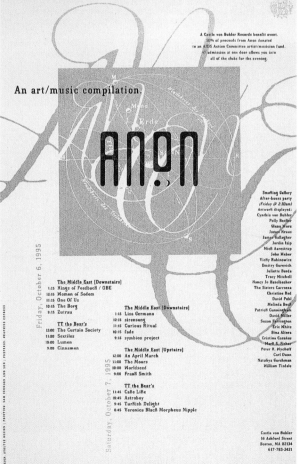

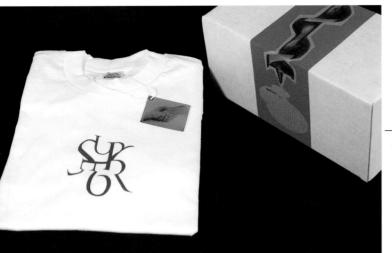

DESIGN   Doug Bartow
PROJECT  Super 6 promotional mailer
TOOLS    Macintosh
FONT     Trajan

This is a promotional piece designed for direct mail. The image of the handshake, which was **screen printed** onto **aluminum flashing,** is a metaphor for an introduction.

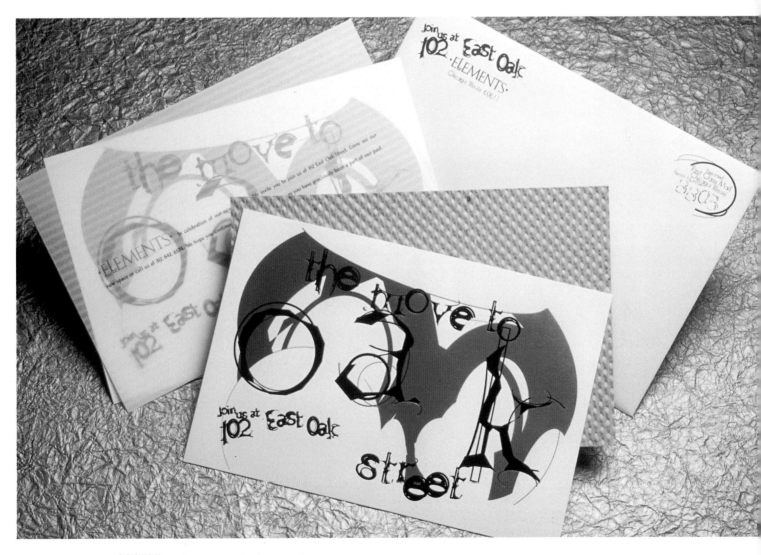

DESIGN   Carlos Segura for Segura, Inc.
PROJECT  Elements relocation project
CLIENT   Elements
TOOLS    QuarkXPress, Adobe Illustrator
FONTS    Finial, Futura

These **moving announcements** for a retail store played on their new address, Oak Street, and therefore were **silkscreened** on oak.

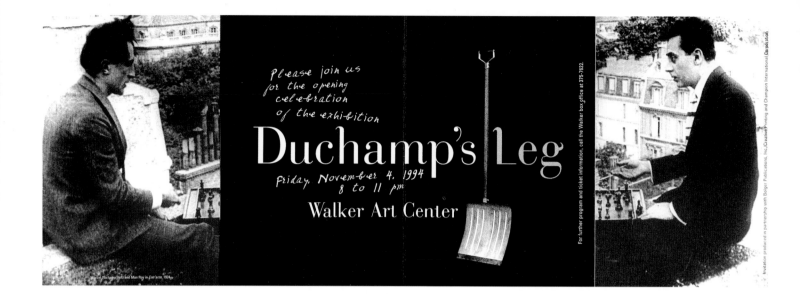

Please join us
for the opening
celebration
of the exhibition

# Duchamp's Leg

Friday, November 4, 1994
8 to 11 pm

## Walker Art Center

For further program and ticket information, call the Walker box office at 375-7622.

DESIGN   Matt Eller for Walker Art Center
PROJECT  Typeface
CLIENT   Marcel
TOOLS    Fontographer on Macintosh
FONT     Bauer Bodoni

This is a **typeface** developed in conjunction with Duchamp's Leg, an exhibition examining **Marcel Duchamp's continuing influence** on subsequent **generations of artists.**
An **equally stoic Bodoni** has now been defaced, albeit cutely.

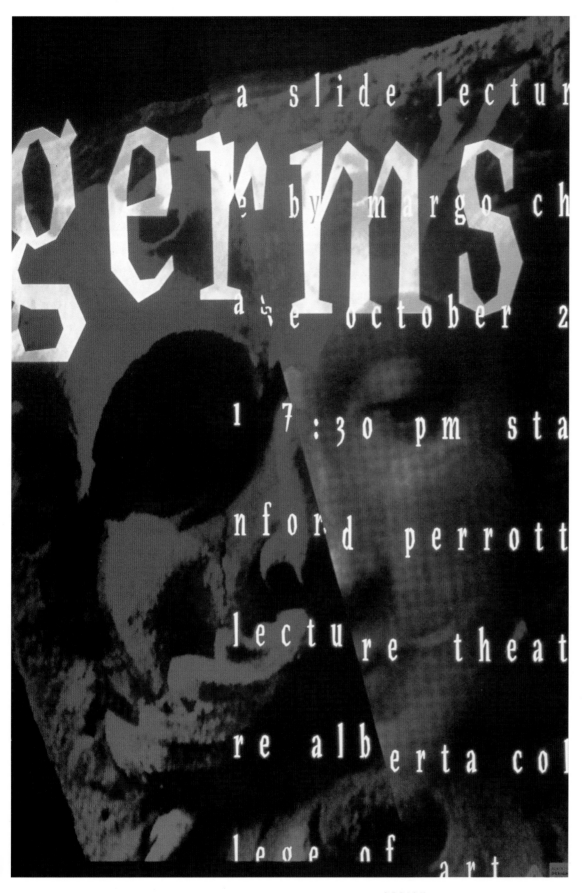

a slide lectur

germs

by margo ch

a e october 2

1 7:30 pm sta

nfo rd perrott

lecture theat

re alberta col

lege of art

DESIGN Margo Chase for Margo Chase Design
TOOLS Fontstudio
FONT Bradley

Designed with no curves at all, this font
was inspired by **Czech woodcut** typefaces.
It's condensed in its original form, but because of the lack
of curves, it "extends" well to create new styles.

DESIGN Carlos Segura for Segura, Inc.
PROJECT Alternative Pick
CLIENT Alternative Pick
TOOLS QuarkXPress, Adobe Illustrator
FONTS Boxspring, Mattress

This is the **1996** version of the **Alternative Pick,** a sourcebook from New York.

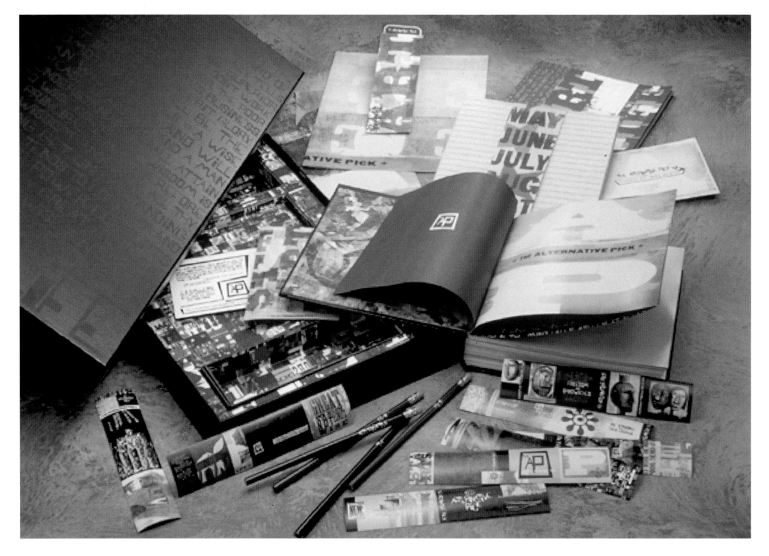

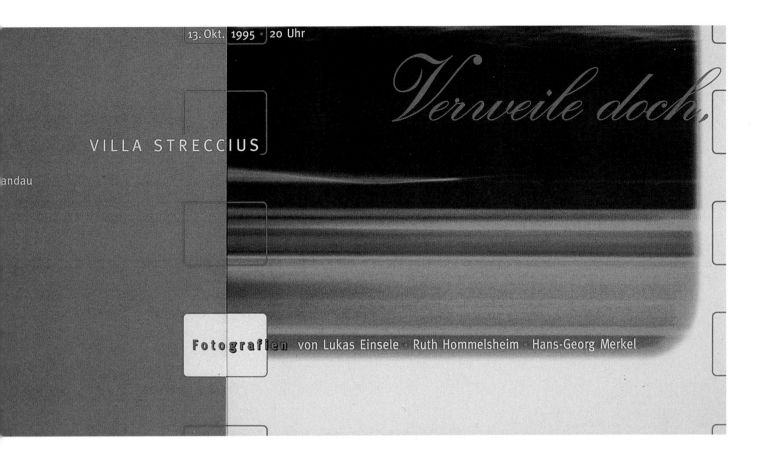

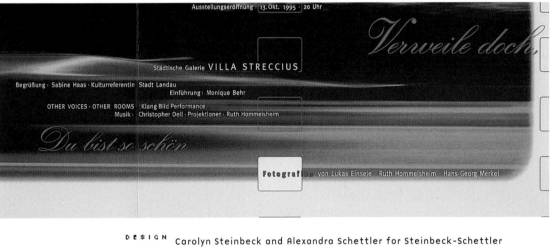

**DESIGN** Carolyn Steinbeck and Alexandra Schettler for Steinbeck-Schettler
**PROJECT** *Verweile doch, Du bist so schön*
**CLIENT** Gallery Villa Strecclus, Landau, Germany
**TOOLS** Adobe Photoshop, QuarkXPress on Macintosh
**FONTS** Künstler Script, Officina

---

The project was an invitation to a photography show.
The project title roughly translates to, "**Linger, you are so beautiful.**"

**DESIGN** Margo Chase for Margo Chase Design
**TOOLS** Fontographer
**FONTS** Box Gothic

Box Gothic was inspired by 1980s **Japanese design**.
The letters all fit into the **same proportion box**.
**There are no curves** and only vertical horizontal lines.

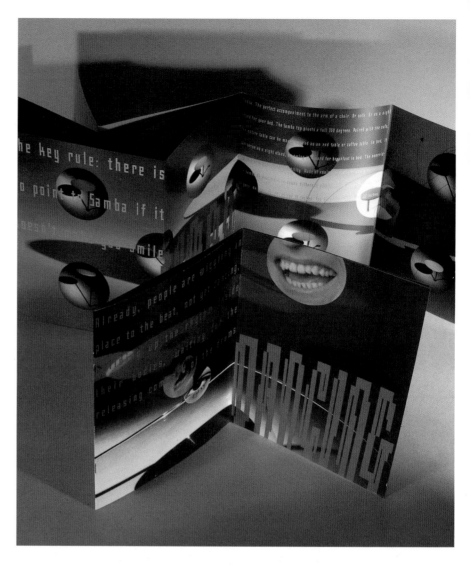

**DESIGN** Margo Chase for Margo Chase Design
**TOOLS** Fontographer
**FONTS** Trajan, OCR

This font was desinged to look like **badly printed or decayed** Roman titling to make a traditional typographic treatment on a CD cover look both **old and contemporary**.
It was created using the **"blend fonts"** filter in Fontographer and then reworked by hand.

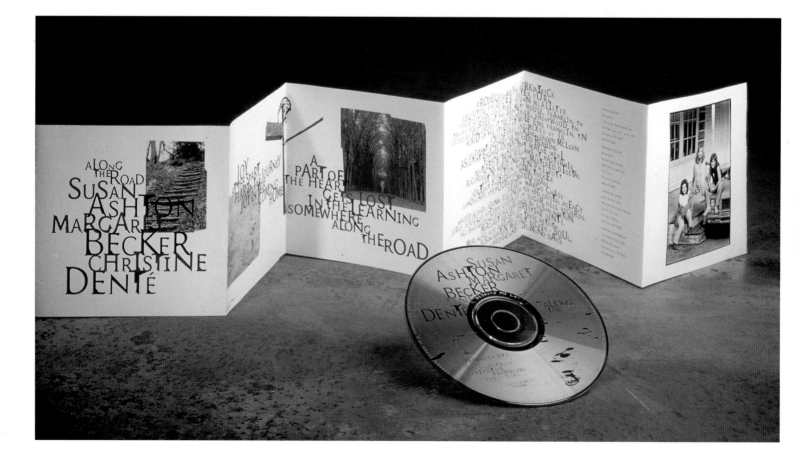

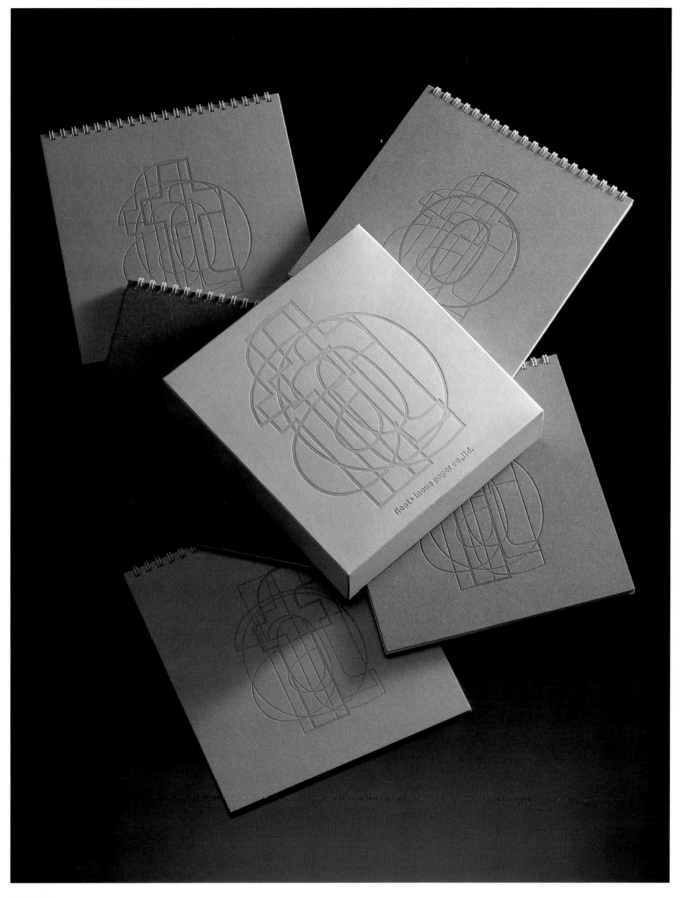

DESIGN  Shuichi Nogami for Nogami Design Office
CLIENT  Inoue Paper Co., Ltd.
TOOLS  Adobe Illustrator on Macintosh
FONTS  Franklin Gothic Demi

"Float" was printed using a **heat treatment process,**
and no ink was necessary.

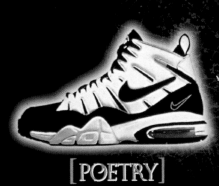

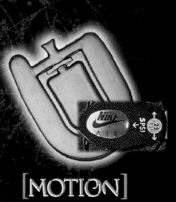

DESIGN Doug Bartow
PROJECT Nike AirMax2 advertisement series
TOOLS Macintosh

The designer used the provided **digital imagery** to create three layouts that present a **series of dichotomies** for the three separate layouts: art/science, poetry/motion, and truth/knowledge.

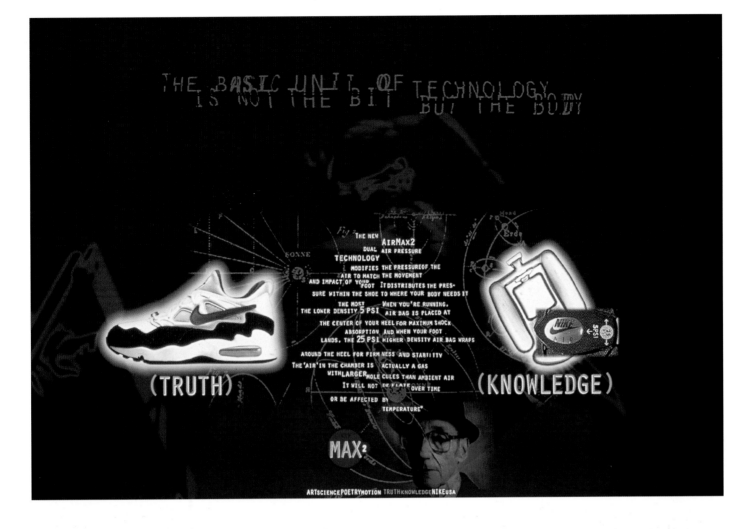

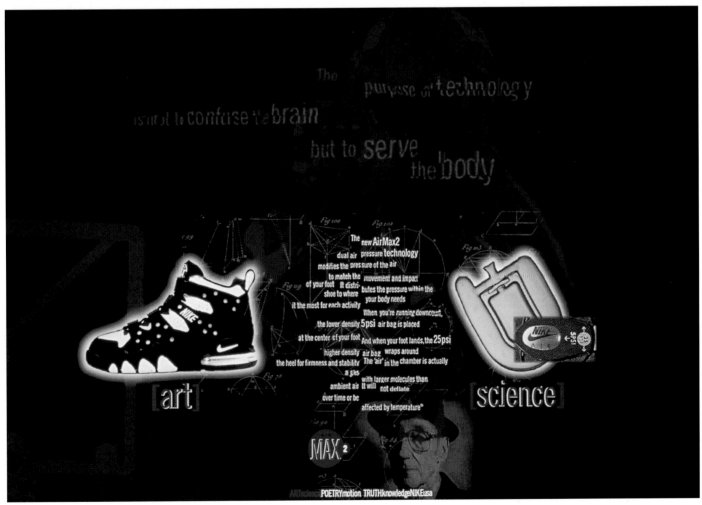

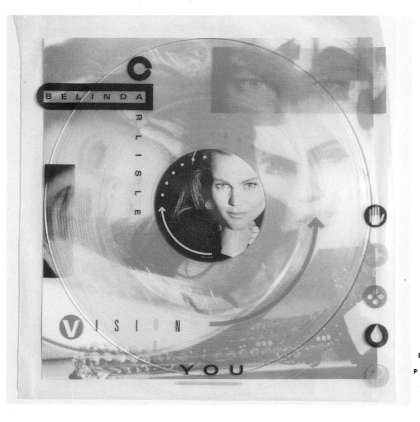

DESIGN    Norman Moore for Design Art, Inc.
PROJECT   Belinda Carlisle—*Vision of You*
CLIENT    Virgin Records
TOOLS     Adobe Photoshop, QuarkXPress, FreeHand on Macintosh
FONT      Univers

This is a **12-inch vinyl music package**, including a transparent disc and a transparent vinyl silkscreened bag.

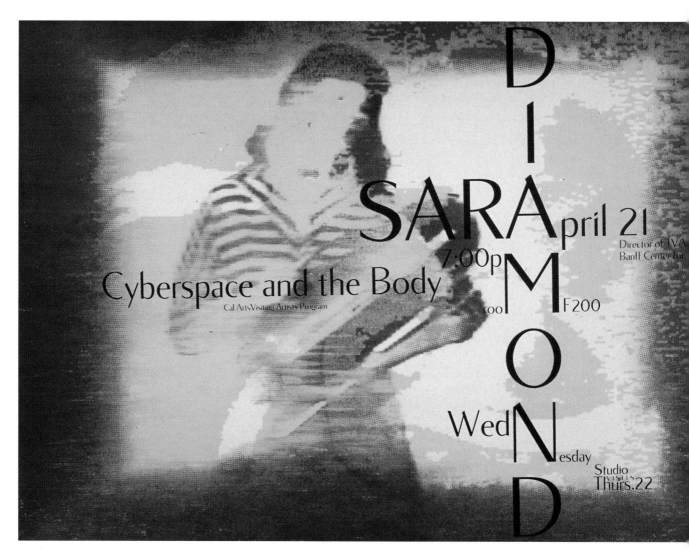

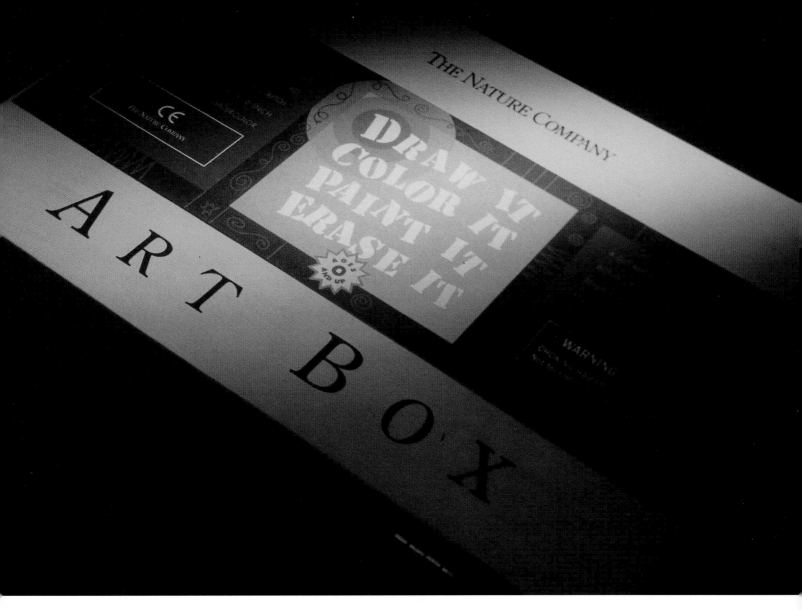

**DESIGN** Mark Sackett, Wayne Sakamoto, James Sakamoto for Sackett Design Associates
**PROJECT** The Nature Company Art Box
**CLIENT** The Nature Company
**TOOLS** QuarkXPress, Adobe Illustrator, Adobe Photoshop on Macintosh
**FONT** Stencil

This box of art supplies for children needed to be **repackaged with a simple label** that could be **hand applied to each box**. The type was rotated at different angles. Filters were also used to create **transparency in the design.**

**DESIGN** James Stoecker and Margo Johnson
**PROJECT** CalArts Arts: Visiting Artist Program
**CLIENT** CalArts Art Department
**TOOLS** FreeHand, Fontographer
**FONT** James Stoecker's Font: Mansonic

The image in the background is so complex that it required **a more structured approach to the type. Playful but classic**, the cross shapes echo from image to text.

directory

Doug Bartow
87 Marshall Street
North Adams, MA 02147

CARE Communications
151 Ellis Street NE
Atlanta, GA 30303

Charles Carpenter Design Studio
2501 Foothill Boulevard #3
La Crescenta, CA 91214

Depke Design
1492 Furnleigh Lane
Chesterton, IN 46304

Design Art, Inc.
6311 Romaine Street #7311
Los Angeles, CA 90038

Giana Illustration and Design
17 Colonial Drive
Simsbury, CT 06086

Graphic Art Studio
Via San Vincenzo, 26
80053 C/MMARE Di Stabia
Italy

Frau Steinbeck Design
Friedelstrasse 40
12047 Berlin
Germany

FUSE, Inc.
483 Moreland Avenue NE, #4
Atlanta, GA 30307

Hans Flink Design, Inc.
224 East 50th Street
New York, NY 10022

International Events
1919 Menalto Avenue
Menlo Park, CA 94025

Kan Tai-keung Design and
Associates, Ltd.
28/F Great Smart Tower
230 Wanchai Road
Hong Kong

Kelly Brother lllustration
5250 Sycamore Grove
Memphis, TN 38120

Deborah Littlejohn
4130 Blaisdell Avenue South
Minneapolis, MN 55403

Malcolm Turk Studios
16 Abingdon Square 2C
New York, NY 10014

Margo Chase Design
2255 Bancroft Avenue
Los Angeles, CA 90039

Matteo Bologna Design NY
142 West 10th Street #2
New York, NY 10014

Mike Salisbury Communications
2200 Amapola Court
Suite 202
Torrance, CA 90501

Mires Design, Inc.
2345 Kettner Boulevard
San Diego, CA 92101

Miriello Grafico, Inc.
419 West G Street
San Diego, CA 92101

Nogami Design Office
5-7-14-103, Nishinakajima
Yodogawa-ku, Osaka 532
Japan

Pentagram Design
204 Fifth Avenue
New York, NY 10010

Peter Piper Graphics
501 Green-Heights
1-7 Midori-Machi
Moriguchi-City, Osaka, 570
Japan

PJ Graphics
4223 Glencoe Avenue #C-203
Marina del Rey, CA 90292

re: salzman design
293 Rabideau Street
Cadyville, NY 12918

Rebeca Méndez Design
Those People
1023 Garfield Avenue
South Pasadena, CA 91030

Red Rockett Design
124 W 24th, Suite 5-D
New York, NY 10011

ReVerb
5514 Wilshire Boulevard #900
Los Angeles, CA 90036

Robert Bak
76-200 Stupsk
Witosa 6/45
Poland

Sackett Design Associates
2103 Scott Street
San Francisco, CA 94115

Segura, Inc.
1110 North Milwaukee Avenue
Chicago, IL 60622

SLIP
4820 North Seeley Avenue
Floor 3
Chicago, IL 60625

Steinbeck-Schettler
Friedelstrasse 40
12047 Berlin
Germany

Stoecker, James
740 16th Avenue
Lenlo Park, CA 94025

Stojan
Pekel 32
62211 Pesnica
Slovenia

Stoltze Design
49 Melcher Street
Fourth Floor
Boston, MA 02210

The Apollo Program
82 East Elm Street
Greenwich, CT 06830

Todd Childers Graphic Design
130 North Grove Street
Bowling Green, OH 43402

Sander van Baalen
INA Boudier Bakker Laan 15-2
3582 VB Utrecht
The Netherlands

Visual Dialogue
429 Columbus Avenue #1
Boston, MA 02116

Walker Art Center
Vineland Place
Minneapolis, MN 55403

index